The Cuban Sandwich

UNIVERSITY PRESS OF FLORIDA

Florida A&M University, Tallahassee
Florida Atlantic University, Boca Raton
Florida Gulf Coast University, Ft. Myers
Florida International University, Miami
Florida State University, Tallahassee
New College of Florida, Sarasota
University of Central Florida, Orlando
University of Florida, Gainesville
University of North Florida, Jacksonville
University of South Florida, Tampa
University of West Florida, Pensacola

The
Cuban
Sandwich

A HISTORY IN LAYERS

**Andrew T. Huse, Bárbara C. Cruz,
and Jeff Houck**

UNIVERSITY PRESS OF FLORIDA

Gainesville • Tallahassee • Tampa • Boca Raton

Pensacola • Orlando • Miami • Jacksonville • Ft. Myers • Sarasota

Publication of this work is made possible by a Sustaining the Humanities through the American Rescue Plan grant from the National Endowment for the Humanities.

27 26 25 24 23 22   6 5 4 3 2 1

ISBN 978-0-8130-6938-8
Library of Congress Control Number: 2022935138

The University Press of Florida is the scholarly publishing agency for the State University System of Florida, comprising Florida A&M University, Florida Atlantic University, Florida Gulf Coast University, Florida International University, Florida State University, New College of Florida, University of Central Florida, University of Florida, University of North Florida, University of South Florida, and University of West Florida.

University Press of Florida
2046 NE Waldo Road
Suite 2100
Gainesville, FL 32609
http://upress.ufl.edu

For our families, for their love and support

Contents

Introduction 1

1. THE PEARL 5

Copeland and Tony Moré Jr., La Segunda Central Bakery (Tampa) 13

Richard Gonzmart, The Columbia Restaurant (Tampa) 18

2. SANDWICHES 24

Claudio Rodríguez, Morrison Meat Packers (Miami) 39

Nicole Valls, Versailles Restaurant (Miami) 42

3. CIGAR CITIES 45

Carlos Gazitua, Sergio's Restaurant (Miami) 58

Gilbert Arriaza Sr. and Gilbert Arriaza Jr., Gilbert's Bakery (Miami) 61

Ignacio Alfonso Jr., El Artesano Restaurant (Union City, New Jersey) 62

4. MAGIC CITIES 65

Norman Van Aken, Chef and Author (Miami) 77

Melinda Lopez, Playwright and Performer (Boston, Massachusetts) 82

Michelle Bernstein, Cafe La Trova (Miami) 84

5. EXILE AND RESILIENCE 89

Dennis Martínez Miranda, Cubanidad 1885 (Las Vegas, Nevada) 107

Carlos Argüelles, The Cuban Sandwich Factory (Belfast, Ireland) 110

6. FEAST AND FAMINE 113

Daniel Figueredo and Rosa Romero, Sanguich de Miami (Miami) 125

Andrew Tambuzzo, The Boozy Pig (Tampa) 131

7. GOING GLOBAL 135

The Staff of Cook's Country: Test Kitchen Chefs 144

Acknowledgments 151
Notes 153
Index 163

The
Cuban
Sandwich

Introduction

Hungry patrons line the long curve of the horseshoe-shaped counter. Standing tall on a small platform behind it, the aproned *lonchero*,[1] or sandwich man, wields his large knife. In quick and efficient movements, he cuts several thin slices from a ham. Using the flat of the blade and a flick of his wrist, he flips the ham slices into a split loaf of long, crusty Cuban bread. He repeats the process with a large roast of pork that has been steeped with the savory flavors of Cuba known as *mojo:* sour orange, garlic, cumin, and more. He then adds a slice or two of Swiss cheese, pickled cucumber, and paints the top face of the sandwich with mustard. Finally, the *lonchero* butters the very top of the sandwich and clamps it into a hot press. With pressure and heat, the flattened layered creation emerges a Cuban sandwich, burnished into a distinctive toasty melt.

When prepared well, the Cuban sandwich enthralls with the first bite, the audible crunch as your teeth shatter the toasted Cuban bread and plunge into the warm fillings inside. Sweet ham, pungent Cuban roast pork, the subtle charm of Swiss cheese, briny pickles, mustard, and sometimes more—are sliced and layered to become one dynamic flavor on the palate. Depending on when and where one orders a Cuban sandwich, the eatery may have added other ingredients. While aficionados debate whether salami belongs on a true Cuban, fewer understand just how mixed-up the ingredients in old *mixto* sandwiches can be. Then there's all the strange things *Americanos* and others have put on their "Cubans."

Miami, Key West, and Tampa have wrangled over the claim to be the Cuban sandwich's true hometown for years. Countless restaurants, bars, and lunch trucks have adopted the sandwich for their menus, along with corporate giants such as McDonald's, Arby's, and Pollo Tropical. In Hollywood, the film *Chef* (2014) vaulted the sandwich into the international limelight. Active interest in the Cuban sandwich online increased twelvefold (1,200 percent) between 2004 and 2018. There are restaurants dedicated to making the sandwich as a specialty across the globe, while Cuban-inspired recipes proliferate online. The Cuban sandwich, conceived by the Cuban people and adopted by the United States, truly belongs to the world now. All the world, it would seem, except for Cuba itself.

The Cuban sandwich seems so simple with store-bought shortcuts but is in fact a series of labor-intensive recipes assembled into a new whole. Anyone making one for an experienced audience must often contend with idiosyncratic expectations for absurdly low prices. Armchair artisans relish in quibbling over their preferences for ingredients, the rights and rites of pressing, condiments, and so on. Sandwich slingers around the world have crafted their own versions in a search for perfection, or at least a living. Ask a hundred locals in Miami or Tampa, and you will get a hundred stories, told with passionate certainty, that their grandfather or local café taught them the proper way—the *only* way—to prepare and eat the sandwich. Journalists and food writers have pondered the story of the Cuban sandwich for decades. Clearly, an examination of the historical record and the sandwich's cultural impact is necessary.

Now at long last there is a chronicle worthy of this outsized sandwich and the people who create it, brought to you by three of the sandwich's most obsessive fans. Dr. Bárbara Cruz is a Cuban American educator, and like most Cubans, she has a serious fixation on food. Jeff Houck is a restaurant marketer with a voracious eye for detail and an insider's perspective of the hospitality business. Andrew Huse is an archivist, historian, and sandwich obsessive who has had a longtime fascination with the Cuban sandwich and its historic roots.

Together, we trace the epic journey of the *mixto, Cubano,* and *medianoche* from hazy origins, through the cafés of Havana, and on to several generations of exiles in new lands. We explore how the crusty creation became a beloved symbol for a displaced people, won the hearts and mouths of America, and claimed a place on the world's stage. Through historic research using sources from Cuba and the United States, we place the sandwich in the context of the Cuban American exile experience and the marketplace of popular culture. We bring the story of the sandwich to life with interviews and profiles of artisans who practice the arts of Cuban bread, ham, roast pork, and more. Finally, readers will find professional tips for creating their own glorious Cuban sandwiches at home, and in the process, honor the journeys of those who made it possible.

Before we get to sandwiches, it would be helpful to briefly review the word itself and its cultural implications. While the Spanish-speaking world generally uses *sándwich* to denote a meal constructed between slices of bread, it also uses other words, such as *bocadillo* (small bite), a term that could refer to a wide range of appetizers. Another common Spanish word for sandwich is *emparedado,* which means "to be walled in or surrounded." The use of *emparedado* was especially championed by people living in Santiago, Cuba, as an alternative to the invasive *Yanqui* word, which Cubans found difficult to pronounce. English speakers make a hard "D" sound by touching their tongues to the ridge between the upper teeth and the hard palate. Spanish speakers make a softer sound by touching their tongues to the back of their upper teeth. To emulate the hard "D," many Cubans substituted a "G" sound, resulting in *sangwich.*

There is some significance to the usage of *emparedado,* not only for being the Spanish word adopted for the sandwich but for its other meaning. Cubans throughout history could deeply identify with an essence being trapped between unyielding pressures. Being a colony in a far-flung empire meant that Cubans spent centuries steeped in the tension between loyalty and independence. Colonists born in Cuba may have been Spanish by lineage, but by virtue of being born in the colonies they were ranked as a lower class, *criollo* (creole), than those born in mainland Spain, known as *peninsulares.* Creoles in search of status would always be caught between the expectations of nobility and the reality of their Cuban birth. The children of mixed-race couples, Afro-Cubans (known then as *mulatos*) were even more socially disadvantaged.

After independence, the unequal and seemingly doomed romance between Cuba and the United States ended during the pressures of the Cold War. Cuba became a pawn of the Soviet Union and the target of an unyielding US trade embargo. Cuban exiles who resettled in the United States may have found safety and prosperity but were condemned to a life suspended between two worlds.

Cubans of all shades and persuasions have known what it feels like to have one's fate determined by people in distant lands, to be trapped or walled in by overwhelming forces, from the sugar market to the Cold War. A Cuban sandwich is made complete, after all, when it is crushed between two hot sheets of metal, hardening its shell until its insides melt and its fat begins to render.

In most of the material written about the sandwich, it is typically represented with a couple of sentences and a short list of store-bought ingredients to assemble. This radically reductive approach strips the sandwich of context, including the people and culture who created it in the first place. Hiding between the thin slices of its fillings are invisible layers of meaning, the spirit of a people, and the story of a nation—the life and times of the Cuban sandwich.

A Note on Research

This book represents an earnest attempt to tell the story of the Cuban sandwich with the limited resources available. Politics and pandemics have complicated research in Cuba itself, and relevant written Cuban sources are scarce in the United States. We encourage others to build upon our efforts when more information becomes readily available.

1

The Pearl

The Pearl of the Antilles

Much like Cuban bread holds the fillings of the sandwich together, history binds this epic story. The creation of what we know as a Cuban sandwich appears to have roughly coincided with the birth of an independent Cuban republic.

In 1492, Christopher Columbus blundered across the Antilles Islands[1] and the New World while looking for Asia. The Spanish Empire conquered Cuba in 1512, using it as a launching pad for the subjugation of much of Central and South America. The cultivation of sugar and tobacco, fueled with African slave labor, made Cuba a vital strategic and economic asset, the coveted Pearl of the Antilles. Governed by bureaucrats an ocean away in Spain, Cubans learned to ignore most imperial decrees and to distrust law and authority. In the 1700s, as much as three-quarters of the tobacco harvest was smuggled out of the country rather than sold to Spanish authorities at fixed prices.

Beginning in the 1760s, slave-cultivated sugar became Cuba's chief export crop. This new direction for the colony promised riches but also tied the fate of the island to an inherently unstable market and an immoral, unsustainable labor system. Much of Cuba's natural, capital, and human resources were devoted to the volatile fortunes of the sugar industry, leaving little for subsistence. As a result, Cuba still struggled with the issue more than two hundred years later, with much of its economic life determined by the international demand for sugar. While the population shot up during the 1800s, the volume of livestock and food crops declined. By the 1890s, Cuba's dependence on imported food sharply increased, along with prices. Life could be difficult on the island, but Cuba was among the Spanish Empire's richest prizes.[2]

The dynamics of race were more fluid in Latin America than in the English-speaking colonial world. In the colonial days, many Afro-Cubans earned their freedom or were born free, and Spanish law recognized their rights. Free blacks dominated several artisan trade guilds and joined local militias. Many Spaniards and *criollos* (Spaniards born in the colonies) had relationships with Afro-Cuban women, many of these unequal by nature, ranging from rape and concubinage to genuine marriage. The dearth of whites left plenty of space for blacks to participate in public life. All these factors gave rise to a culture that, while not color-blind, was less sharply segregated than many others at the time.[3]

Havana became Cuba's biggest window to the rest of the world and a powerful cultural incubator. The port city produced hard wooden pegs called *clavijas* used for shipbuilding, an industry with deep roots in Havana. The people soon turned the pegs into a signature percussion instrument, the *clave,* which is used to create the bedrock rhythm inherent in much of Cuban dance music.[4] Havana took on a more cosmopolitan character in the 1800s, with more hotels, cafés and its first steamship route in 1821, establishing a connection with New Orleans. Nightlife was decidedly raucous, with the exception of the nicer theaters and the *Filarmónica.*[5]

Cuba's political culture reached a fever pitch in the mid-1800s. A new strident nationalism was reflected in the rise of *lectores,* the readers hired to recite news and literature to the workers in cigar factories. Initially, *lectores* were typically affiliated with the newspapers printed by labor unions based in Havana. Later, workers in a given factory hired their own *lectores* and chose the material to be read. The voices of political and labor ferment gave rise to a new consciousness, the dream of a nation yet to be born.[6]

Cuban Cuisine

The renowned Cuban anthropologist Fernando Ortiz compared his nation's identity to the cooking of *ajiaco,* a stew of Spanish beef, Native Indian *ají* (chile peppers), and starchy tubers such as yuca and yams that were associated with African slave food. Taíno natives prepared *ajiaco* originally in a hole in the ground lined with leaves, probably banana. The ingredients cooked slowly, simmered by the sun. Over time, members of the tribe might take some to eat and add more ingredients to the stew. In this way, *ajiaco* might cook for many days or even weeks at a time. The strong flavor of the chiles had the virtue of masking the flavors of spoiled ingredients. Some Cubans interpret their culture as an ongoing *ajiaco,* which is never fully cooked or quite complete.[7]

To fully understand Cuban cuisine, it is best to know something beyond ingredients and demographics to contemplate the spirit of the people. In his *Global Handbook* devoted to Cuba, Ted Henken writes, "Cuban etiquette revolved around the national characteristics of boisterousness and loquaciousness, sensuality and secularity, jocularity and mockery, ambition and modernity. The most distinctive social characteristic shared by Cubans is a deep sense of hospitality. Cubans also tend to hold conversations at an unusually high volume and are masters at the art of conversation, often holding forth for hours."[8]

Antonio Benítez-Rojo, one of Cuba's literary greats, identified the two conflicting natures in the island's history, known as *Cuba Grande* and *Cuba Pequeña* (Big and Little Cuba, respectively). Authoritarianism, pride, brutality, and sugar plantations represented the Big Cuba of the financial elites but did not represent the soul of the common people, or Little Cuba. The true Cuban spirit, also known as *lo cubano* or "the Cuban way," could only be found in Little Cuba. The most famous and durable creations of Cuban culture would not be passed down by elites but percolated insistently from below. Even Cuba's food was traditionally produced on small-scale *sitio* farms, often run by ex-slaves and their descendants who were fiercely proud of their humble estates.[9]

Some scholars have traced the origins of an independent Cuba to the rich body of literature produced there beginning in the mid-1800s. Among a flowering of revolutionary thought, the upstart nation's earliest cookbooks were vital in forging an identity apart from Spain's. *Comida criolla* (Creole food) became an important facet of Cuban nationalism in the 1850s. Advocates of independence renounced Spain and its system of sugar and slaves, while extolling Cuban folk traditions, especially food. Cuban cookbooks arose along with the island's literacy rate and growing middle class, documenting the depth and local variety of the national cuisine at the time. Cuban nationalists held up ingredients such as *boniato* (also known as white sweet potato), plantains, and yuca, and recipes such as *ajiaco* as being distinctly Cuban rather than Spanish. True *criolla* cuisine included indigenous and African influences.[10]

If the primordial bedrocks of Cuban food can be found in *ajiaco,* other vital ingredients made a more dynamic cuisine possible. Influences from Spain were strongly felt on the Cuban table. Previously a luxurious import, rice became such a staple in Cuba that it is difficult to imagine the island's food without it. Chinese railroad laborers helped to popularize rice cultivation in the mid-1800s. Cubans embraced it with the passion of the newly converted, and it was soon served with virtually every meal, including dishes that already boasted plenty of starch. The crop also made Spanish-style *arroz con pollo* (chicken with yellow rice) attainable for more Cubans, who adopted it as a favorite, as it was across most of Latin America and the Spanish-speaking Caribbean. *Congrí* is a *criolla* rice favorite, mixing red beans with rice, a simple dish with countless variations. Mixed black beans and rice are popularly known as *Moros y Cristianos* (Moors and Christians), referring to the mixing of black and white ingredients.[11]

Cubans often prefer meat over seafood, especially beef, pork, and more recently, chicken. Iconic dishes include *ropa vieja* ("old clothes," a braised shredded beef dish) and *picadillo* (a dish of ground beef simmered with tomato and more), invariably accompanied by black beans, white rice, plantains, and tubers such as yuca. Pork had been a staple in Cuba since the days of Columbus's second transatlantic voyage in 1493, when the conquistador introduced pigs to the New World. Rough and hearty, the Spanish pigs had no natural enemies on the island and multiplied freely. They quickly became the protein of choice for the slow-cooked *barbacoa* of the local Taíno Indians. From hogs, Cubans cured ham and prepared *lechón,* slow-roasted pork that may or may not be made from suckling pig, hence the reference to milk (*leche*) in its name. Cuban *lechón* is usually marinated in a sour orange, lime, garlic, and oregano sauce called *mojo.*

It seems only natural that ham and *lechón* would later be used as the basis for a sandwich that bears the island's name. It is important to note that none of the scholars discussing traditional Cuban food include any sandwiches, let alone the *mixto* or "Cuban" sandwich, in their discussions.[12]

Cuba Libre

Spain had lost most of its vast empire in the early 1800s, but Cuba and Puerto Rico remained colonies of the crown. Cuba's continuing fealty to Spain won approval as the "Ever-Faithful Isle" from Madrid, but there was a limit to the people's loyalty. Imperial bankruptcy prompted crushing taxes and trade regulations, and Cubans soon demanded more representation and autonomy. Periodic slave revolts and bloody repression further destabilized the colony. Spanish authorities routinely imprisoned or exiled political dissidents and advocates of independence. Known as *El Exilio* (The Exile),[13] the Cuban diaspora began as early as 1823. That is when Spanish authorities sentenced Cuban religious leader, humanitarian, and political advocate Father Félix Varela y Morales to death for being too critical of Madrid. Varela y Morales fled Cuba for a life of exile and distinguished charity work in New York City. The first significant numbers of Cuban immigrants came to the United States in 1832, with many settling in Key West.[14]

Vexed by the simmering issues of independence and slavery, much of Cuba revolted against Spanish rule during the inconclusive Ten Years' War (1868–1878). Starting in 1868, a steady stream of exiles fled the violence and hardship to Key West, which quickly transformed the small island into Florida's biggest city and the capital of cigar production in the United States. Although the struggle failed to achieve independence, the rebellion left a legacy of Cuban exile communities across the Western Hemisphere. In 1879, just after the war's end, an estimated fifty thousand Cubans lived in the United States, with about 2,400 in Key West.[15] To Spain's chagrin, Cuba's economy (and exiles) gradually reoriented itself toward the growing wealth of the United States.[16]

Collectively and individually, the exile community was mobile, resilient, and rather prosperous; it was composed of intellectuals, skilled workers, and laborers alike. Because the rebellion lasted for so long, many Cubans became accustomed to the idea of indefinite exile, but they were determined to have a voice in the future of their budding island nation. *El Exilio* became a respected rite of patriotism understood by all politically active Cubans.[17] The independence movement rapidly regrouped from an isolated peasant and slave rebellion into a revolution that tapped into people's hopes for a more equitable Cuba. The ideals of the exile community were best expressed by José Martí, the foremost intellectual leader of the Cuban independence movement.[18]

Beginning in 1895, Cuban rebels outfought and outran the Spanish during the Cuban War for Independence, but the struggle took a terrible toll on the people and economy. The United States went to war with Spain in April 1898, about two months after the *USS Maine* exploded in Havana Harbor, although economic and geopolitical concerns had already made a conflict likely. Unwilling to allow another expansionist country to control the island should Spain withdraw, US strategists also resisted the idea of an independent Cuba. By calling it the Spanish-American War (1898), diplomats and historians at the time managed to exclude the pretext for the war in the first place: the struggles of Cubans and Filipinos for independence from empires.

The Spanish-American War lasted from April until August, and US troops invaded, ostensibly to aid the Cuban rebels. After fighting over Cuba, Puerto Rico and the Philippines, the United States seized most of the remnants of Spain's overseas empire. The sometimes disorderly behavior of US troops can be better understood by the potent cocktail that was popularized during the war. The *Cuba Libre* (Free Cuba), made with Cuban rum, American Coca-Cola, and lime, had three active ingredients: alcohol, caffeine, and cocaine. After a few of those, drinkers might feel that they could conquer the whole world, not just the isle of Cuba (cocaine was phased out of the Coca-Cola recipe in 1903). Even if Coca-Cola wasn't readily available to soldiers in the field, many of them never left the mainland and spent much of their free time seeking out beverages.

While Cuba was not formally made a US territory, such as Puerto Rico, Guam, and the Philippines, it did not attain complete independence, either. The peace settlement ensured that Cuba would become a dependency of the United States and therefore did little to mollify advocates of true Cuban independence.

Enter the *Yanqui*

"Cuba is simply over-run with Americans of all ages," the *New York Times* observed, "of all conditions of life, of all professions, and of no professions. Years ago the rush was to the west of the United States: now the tide has turned southward to Cuba." In 1899, an ice cream parlor in Havana printed newspaper ads specifically aimed at "Ladies" (in English).[19]

While some visitors from the north took interest in Cuban food, they usually viewed anything unfamiliar with suspicion. One American housewife living in Cuba observed in 1905,

> Cuban cooking is greasy and mysterious. It is unsuited for delicate digestion, and is not always appetizing in appearance, although many of the dishes are excellent, and one soon learns what to avoid. The Cuban cook can prepare rice as no American domestic [worker] can ever hope to. It comes to the table a fluffy mass, white and dry, with each grain distinct, and with a flavor which makes it popular from the first tasting in the transplanted family.[20]

Cuba's hospitality industry expanded to accommodate the steady stream of *Americano* investors, tourists, and new residents. In 1899 and 1900, well-financed entrepreneurs from the United States had a keen advantage in opening hotels and other businesses with names like the American Tea Room, the Manhattan Bar, the Gay Broadway Café, the New England Bar, the Greater New York Café, the American Soda Shop, and so on.[21]

Yanqui[22] businessmen brought more than their money and language with them. The new proprietors of the Café Washington from *El Norte* refused to serve dark-skinned Cubans. When authorities closed the café, the owners un-

By the time of its independence, Cuba was home to countless cafés and street vendors who served food and drink with a distinctly Cuban identity. This café scene is from Matanzas in the 1920s. *Havana, Cuba, the Tropical Paradise of the West Indies*, circa 1925.

successfully appealed the case to the Cuban Supreme Court, which rebuked the idea of racial segregation.[23]

A new vibrant Cuba was emerging from out of the shadows of Spanish rule. The people longed for modernity and independence, for baseball instead of bull-fights. As a festive and social Caribbean people, Cubans even today still enjoy long walks through the city or town square. The Sunday promenade, especially in Havana, became a social staple, and the accompanying snack was practically a sacrament. Long walks led to chance meetings and long conversations, which required more food and refreshments along the way.

In addition to the delights of cafés and bakeries, street food was a category all its own in the new Cuba. Hand-held treats and moveable feasts satisfied the people's penchant for snacking between meals. To avoid the heat of the tropical sun, Cubans tended to go out to socialize late into the night. There was seemingly no occasion that could not be improved with a profusion of fritters, empanadas, pies, tamales, turnovers, croquettes, rolls, and tarts. While street foods and hand-held treats existed before independence, they came into their own quickly after. The cheapest snacks could be found at the meat and produce stands run by Chinese immigrants that seemed to supply every park and public space.[24]

Cuban cuisine flourished under the early republic, but the fortunes of most ordinary people remained precarious. The war against Spain achieved an imperfect independence in which Cuba had seemingly exchanged one imperial master for another. Self-interest motivated the United States–led reconstruction program in Cuba. The new republic basked in the sunlight of *Yanqui* investment but also dwelled in its shadows. In a less formal manner of dominance, the products and language from the north penetrated Cuban culture quickly. It began before the war in the middle and upper classes' habit of using baseball jargon. A Cuban journalist noted in 1905, "'Base ball' it seems has been the precursor to the intervention."[25]

The dynamic economic energy of the United States fueled Cuba's remarkable recovery from its utterly ruined state after the war with Spain. The high price of sugar during and after World War I helped in the recovery as well. This rebound came at a steep price. United States corporations and investors quickly bought up 60 percent of the Cuban countryside in the decades after independence. Cubans could only look on as the volatile global sugar market whipsawed from one extreme to the next in what they called "The Dance of the Millions." Even outside of the moribund Spanish Empire, Cubans found that their fortunes were still being decided by faraway financiers.[26]

Independence and its aftermath did not conjure the golden age that many Cubans had hoped for. The great sugar estates consolidated further with US investment, forcing more peasants off the land and stunting the growth of the middle class. The Cuban state had inherited the Spanish tendency toward civic corruption, bribery, and cronyism, which was not dispelled by US occupation and quickly became fully enmeshed into the workings of the state. Personalities stood in for principles, and elections became fraudulent power-grabs for the spoils of office to distribute to family and friends. Soon, politicians settled disputes with violence and assassination.[27]

Copeland and Tony Moré Jr.,
La Segunda Central Bakery (Tampa)

Copeland Moré shrugged when asked how he got into the family bakery business. "It must be in our blood." But that makes his occupation seem a matter of fate. Real life was much more unpredictable. No one thought he would wind up running La Segunda Central Bakery. His father Tony has a similar story, but they now find themselves running a century-old bakery that produces superior Cuban bread. Bakeries in Cuba don't make it this way anymore.

Sometime around 1900, Copeland's great-grandfather Juan Moré brought his Cuban bread recipe to Tampa scribbled on a piece of paper. Born in Catalonia, Moré left for Cuba in the late 1890s, perhaps as a conscript in the Spanish army. It is said that he deserted in Cuba and left for Florida during the Spanish-American War of 1898. Moré wandered up Florida's east coast to St. Augustine but did not settle down until he arrived in Tampa. He became a partner in several bakeries, eventually buying out his associates at La Primera de Ybor (The First of Ybor) bakery on Eighth Avenue in 1915. That location burned down, and the new bakery became known as La Segunda Central.

Juan's sons Tony and Raymond took over the family business from their father and passed it on to their own sons of the same names. In 1970, Tony Jr. received a PhD degree in chemistry at Florida State University and took a job with an engineering firm in Tampa. When he was laid off, he briefly took work as a teacher at Mulberry High School. His father had become swamped at the bakery and asked Tony for help. Raymond Jr. relieved his father as well. Reticent by nature, Tony ran the production and accounting, while Raymond maintained the equipment and was the face of the business. The young brothers brought in computers to manage the business and gradually expanded their clientele. Most importantly, they never compromised the quality of their product.

Time-intensive techniques, the skill required of the bakers, and the strict recipe make quality Cuban bread production a manifold challenge. During its first seventy years or so, La Segunda was one of many bakeries making Cuban bread in town. As the quality of competition decreased, La Segunda became prominent as one of the very last producers of old-fashioned Cuban bread in Tampa, and perhaps the world. The owners acknowledge that none of it would be possible without the bakery's crew of dedicated artisans. "We've recruited and retained the best. They really know what they're doing."

The Cuban bread originally popularized in Tampa is a type of *pan de agua* (or water bread) with several distinctive features. Preserving a century-old custom, Tampa's best bakers still use the palmetto leaf to crown each loaf. In 1905, the *St. Louis Republican* wrote that Cuban bread was "excellent in quality. The shape of the loaf is always the same—long, narrow, and flat. Americans will find a bit of what seems to be brown paper adhering to the top of the loaf. Each baker purchases daily a number of green banana [palmetto] leaves, a strip of which is fastened to the top of each loaf, for the purpose of preventing the bread from rising too high in the heat of the oven."

Raymond Moré observes about the leaf, "It allows the loaf to blossom out, split up, and lets the gas inside open the bread up so it becomes a lot airier inside. It keeps the crust outside but the nice soft dough inside."

Most Cuban bakeries developed with more modern baking techniques. Raymond described the differences between Cuban bread baked at La Segunda Bakery and typical Cuban bread,

> After we apply steam and we get the dough proofed, we put it in front of the ovens with fans on it. The fans will dry it and actually create a paper-thin crust on it and that's what gives it that flakiness. Once it hits the oven

The palmetto leaves that crown every loaf of La Segunda Central Bakery's bread are one of several heritage techniques that have been preserved during more than a century of business in Tampa. Chip Weiner Photographic Arts.

The crustiness of La Segunda's Cuban bread is the result of proofing in warm air and being cooked directly in the hearth. Chip Weiner Photographic Arts.

and that high heat it immediately gets real crusty, thin like an eggshell. When it hits that hearth, that's when it gets the crust, it opens up and becomes a beautiful loaf of bread.

When you put a lot of bread on a pan it does not work as well as putting directly into the oven. [Others are] interested in the high volume and the profit part, which I can understand, so most of their bread is machine-made. They're mostly automated and they use pans. The bread draws away the heat in the pan, so it's lost the intensive heat that gives it the bounce. It becomes a pan bread, like a hamburger bun or hoagie.

Here, we take each individual loaf and put them one at a time into the hearth, just like baking a pizza, a hot hearth. Lot of bread isn't even split on top, but like a giant hoagie, it comes a lot softer and doesn't have the texture. It's completely different. It gives us a niche in the market that they can't fill because their bread does not compare to ours.

When the bakery first opened in 1915, Juan sold bread to the small Café Columbia down the street beginning in 1915. The Columbia has since grown into a massive restaurant with outlying locations and a massive appetite for bread. It even tried making bread at its own bakery, but abandoned the enterprise and relied on other vendors. When Tony and Raymond Moré—the grandsons of Juan—agreed to supply the Columbia with bread again in 1992, the small bakery worked at capacity to meet demand. Several years later, La Segunda created stable and delicious frozen Cuban bread for the restaurant group, halving the size to eighteen inches for easier shipping. It took many months of trial and error to find the perfect formula, first producing partially baked bread, later replacing it with a fully cooked product. When Tony received a call from Adela Gonzmart, the family's matriarch, he assumed there must have been a problem with the bread. Instead, Adela thanked Tony for supplying such a dependable product far from home.

Adela's praise deeply touched the Morés, who were thrilled to be supplying the Columbia system. What they didn't realize was that they had taken a major step toward national exposure. Aside from being Florida's oldest restaurant and the largest Spanish eatery in the United States, the Columbia enlisted its food distributors to ship the product, making a hyper-local specialty available to restaurants virtually anywhere in the country.

Today, La Segunda counts several Florida chains on its roster of clients, including Beef O'Brady's and Larry's Giant Subs. When Hurricane Grill and Wings ran a Cuban sandwich special using La Segunda's bread, it became an overnight hit and the latest addition to its menu. These chains have opened new doors for the bakery. For example, according to its franchise agreement, each new Beef O'Brady's must be stocked with La Segunda bread for its Cuban and prime rib sandwiches. A new location in Phoenix provides a guaranteed consumer for the distributor, making La Segunda's bread available to other smaller players in the area. Copeland said, "Beef O'Brady's really has created pockets for us that we can market to. Seattle has become a great market for us." Sysco also carries their bread into Alaska, another growing market. Instead of burying smaller operations such as La Segunda, food distributors have made its bread available to new far-flung clients.

In 2008, Copeland Moré worked in commercial real estate finance when the housing bubble burst. At the time, his uncle Raymond was edging toward retirement from the family bakery. Taking a look at the ledgers, Copeland saw signs of promise, but balked at the meager $500 marketing budget. The business had "a small feel" with great potential and he was intrigued.

"Don't do it," his father Tony insisted. "It's 24–7." But Copeland was undeterred and kept asking questions. "You're nuts," came his father's reply. "You're gambling that we're going to make it work." In 2009, convincing his father that he was earnest (if insane), Copeland joined La Segunda and they bought out Raymond. "He's taken it ten times further than we could have," Tony said of his son.

Three generations of La Segunda Bakery family in the Ybor City section of Tampa, Florida: Anthony, Copeland, and Tony Moré surrounded by their signature Cuban bread, circa 1985. Courtesy La Segunda Central Bakery.

While Copeland cannot improve upon his family's Cuban bread, he and his father have nudged the business forward. For starters, they created a website and activated social media profiles. With a new overhead dough proofer, they doubled production to more than 18,000 loaves in three daily shifts. There's even talk about developing frozen guava pastries and different varieties of bread. Copeland would even like to experiment with restoring lard to the Cuban bread recipe, which had been replaced with shortening long ago.

Despite the dilapidated neighborhood, dearth of parking, and lack of tables or dining counters, the original bakery has maintained a steady retail presence in Ybor City. Copeland and Tony renovated the space in 2012 and have opened bakery-cafés in the wealthier climes of South Tampa and St. Petersburg.

Copeland doesn't miss his life as a realtor. "I really love this," he says. "Ask my wife, I'm so much happier when I get home." He loves working with his father and extended bakery family, many of whom he grew up with. Most of all, Moré looks forward to earning some respect for hearth-baked Cuban bread. "There's a lot more to teach the rest of the country," he muses.

Richard Gonzmart,
The Columbia Restaurant (Tampa)

The food of our memories is powerful stuff. The flavors, the aromas, and the places where we consumed them combine to taunt our taste buds and haunt our daydreams.

Fourth-generation restaurateur Richard Gonzmart knows this. When he assumed leadership at his family's Columbia Restaurant, opened in 1905, the signature sandwich sold well, but he craved the version he remembered eating as a boy. Over the years, the sandwich just tasted . . . different. So in 2007, Gonzmart began a quest to remake the sandwich using the recipe his grandfather, Casimiro Hernandez Jr., served to customers in Tampa's Ybor City neighborhood. He had no idea how difficult and expensive it would be to recapture that taste of history.

As anyone researching foodways knows, documentation can be elusive when chasing an origin story through the haze of myth, memories, and emotions. That certainly was true for Gonzmart. He's well-known for cherishing any and all family heirlooms and Columbia restaurant memorabilia. His father Cesar's motorcycle and violin and his mother Adela's piano and wedding dress are on display in a dining room adjacent to the Columbia. His family's photos are archived in an online collection at the University of South Florida Libraries. The Columbia's history mirrors that of Tampa's development, so the fifteen-dining-room, 1,700-seat Spanish-Cuban restaurant has become a time capsule of sorts offering glimpses of the city's rich, immigrant-fueled food history.

Earlier generations, who had no idea what the Columbia's future impact would be, didn't keep menus for at least the first thirty years. The humble Saloon Columbia opened in 1903, and by the 1920s, Prohibition forced the family to hide the liquor and operate as a restaurant. The oldest menu Gonzmart found was from the late 1930s, which included a Cuban "mixto" sandwich. Then he found a copy of his grandfather's recipe, published in 1941. But even that did not include particulars, since restaurant competition was fierce and no one wanted to tip their hand.

"Whatever they did print was always wrong," he said. "'We don't want to tell them how we really make it.' It was asinine. I think a public relations person did it, not understanding that the quantities of some things were crazy."

When he was a boy in the late 1950s, the Columbia had a *ventanita* in the front facing Seventh Avenue, Ybor City's main east-west street. The restaurant had glass-front refrigerators where passing motorists could drive by and see the

Richard Gonzmart, "fourth-generation caretaker" of the family-owned Columbia Restaurant Group in Tampa, reinvented the flagship restaurant's Cuban sandwich to go back to the original recipe from 1915 that relied on house-prepared ham, roast pork, and imported Genoa salami with black peppercorns. Courtesy Columbia Restaurant Group.

ham, the roast pork, salami, and cheese. Worker Luis Garcia, who worked at the Columbia for thirty-seven years, made sandwiches in that window that at one point in time cost seventy-five cents.

In the post–World War II boom years, the restaurant would turn out Cuban sandwiches at the rate of four hundred a day on weekdays and as many as seven hundred on Sundays, when people ordered forty or fifty at a time for picnics. Ángel Fernández had the job of slicing enough meat for the day and night shifts. For weekdays, he'd slice eighty-five pounds of smoked Virginia hams, sixty pounds of roast pork or sixty pounds of turkey (back then, marinated pork was used when the turkey wasn't available), fifteen pounds of Swiss cheese and fifteen pounds of Genoa salami. Later years saw the turkey fade as a sandwich ingredient as roast pork became more popular.

After assembly, the sandwiches were heated sixteen at a time in an oven for six minutes to make the Cuban bread crispy. In the 1960s, the Columbia employed

In old Havana, the Cuban "mixed" sandwiches contained all manner of ingredients, including various kinds of hard chorizo, Spanish *salchichón,* and other tangy meats. In Tampa, salami became the favored third meat for the sandwich and appears with its sister ingredients at the Columbia Restaurant. Chip Weiner Photographic Arts.

electrically heated sandwich presses, likely inspired by the practice in Miami. Richard's father stacked heavy dinner plates on the press to get the sandwiches to a plank-like thickness. Over the decades, the restaurant took shortcuts on ingredients and preparation in the interest of saving time and money. It was easier to let someone else marinate and slow-roast the pork. Deboning the hams before glazing required skillful labor. The ham bones might be used for the restaurant's famous Spanish Bean Soup, but butchers cost money.

"Those are the kind of mistakes people make, including us," Gonzmart said. "You change what made you famous in favor of speed." In a town full of Cuban sandwiches, the reputation of the Columbia's version dimmed. In the mid-2000s, a Tampa food historian told Gonzmart the truth: Of the top ten Cubans in Tampa, the Columbia's was not among them.

"I wasn't going to argue. He was right. We did use shortcuts. We used a different ham. We used a different pork. Everyone has a different thought about what the sandwich should be. I went to a recipe I found from my grandfather."

Propelled by the revelation, Gonzmart set out to remake the sandwich top to bottom, which is crucial, since he considers the Cuban's architecture vitally important to delivering maximum flavor and satisfaction. Make the sandwich incorrectly and he can tell within one bite. "I don't have to take it apart to know it's made wrong. I can taste the difference." A diagram of the sandwich's construction is posted in the kitchen for staff to use as a guide.

Per his specifications, every Columbia Original Cuban Sandwich should be built between a sliced 9-inch loaf of La Segunda Central Bakery bread. La Segunda has been baking for more than one hundred years and the Columbia has purchased loaves since the family-owned bakery opened. Some of the ovens used at La Segunda for baking the bread were bought from Gonzmart's father during his relatively brief stint owning a bakery in Ybor City. In exchange, the Columbia paid three cents less a loaf.

On the bottom slice, a layer of sliced glazed baked ham. The restaurant had been buying bolo hams from a Miami provider. Gonzmart went in search of more flavorful products, doing blind tastings to follow his taste buds. That led to

Note how hot pressing has burnished La Segunda's crusty Cuban bread into a crunchy, flaky delicacy at the Columbia Restaurant.

Wisconsin, where he toured the facilities at Hillshire Farms to inspect how they made hearthstone hams, the same variety hotels use for serving ham steaks. The restaurant now buys from family-owned Compart Family Farms in Wisconsin, which also supplies pork for the Columbia Restaurant Group's fourteen locations and six restaurant concepts.

Key to the Cuban sandwich's ham: It has to have fat for flavor, but not too much. Gonzmart insisted the kitchen return to the old-school ways of scoring the exterior of each boneless ham with a knife and glazing before baking. That hint of sweetness counterbalances the saltiness of the ham.

On top of the sandwich's ham layer rests sliced roasted mojo pork. Again, shortcuts over the years had the pork marinated and roasted by an outside vendor. Instead, Gonzmart invested in a $30,000 oven that allowed the Columbia to roast the mojo pork more efficiently. He chose the Compart pork over less expensive brands partly because of the marbling and the water weight hidden in lesser-quality prepared products.

On top of the pork layer: Four slices of Genoa salami with peppercorns. To refurbish this ingredient, he had to source the salami from Italy. Domestic salamis didn't have the peppercorns that are visible when you make each slice. That bit of peppery flavor is subtle but adds a new dimension.

"It's the difference between being great and good," he says.

Perched on the salami are squared slices of Swiss cheese. The vendors may have changed over the years but the creaminess of the Swiss does not. Whatever the kitchen uses must be pliable enough to melt when heated in a sandwich press.

Each sandwich gets two dill pickle sandwich chips sliced to an exact thickness and then a top layer of bread coated on the inside with yellow mustard. This is crucial. Put the mustard on the bottom slice of bread and it will coat the tongue. On top, it allows the mustard to complement the other flavors and bloom in the roof of the mouth. Gonzmart tested more than a dozen varieties before settling on French's Classic Yellow Mustard.

Once assembled, the sandwich heads to a press, where the top slice's exterior gets a slathering of butter to make the already-crispy loaf even crispier. Pressing isn't required, though. However the customer prefers it is how the sandwich is made. A sign in the kitchen provides all the direction for guest requests: "Yes, We Can."

After pressing for about eight minutes, or until the cheese is melted, the sandwich is sliced corner-to-corner to form two triangles. Again, this is important to Gonzmart.

"You eat from the point down," he said. "You don't eat from the other side. Why are you holding the little point and eating the big part? Then when you eat it with the bottom, you're able to enjoy the crunchiness and the crust that was toasted and savor the flavor. It just tastes different."

He usually defers to the guests' wishes. But one day, he saw a blogger eat the sandwich from the middle. Gonzmart couldn't help himself.

"I had to say, 'Let me tell you this: That's the wrong way you're eating the sandwich. You're not going to enjoy it the same. It's built this way for a reason. It rewards you every time you bite. The more you eat, it feels like a bigger sandwich.'"

The end result is that after The Original Cuban Sandwich debuted on the Columbia's menu in its reengineered version, sales for the item increased forty percent in the first six months. The Columbia Restaurant's menu is replete with Spanish and Cuban classics, succulent meat and seafood. The "1905" Salad and premium sangria are both popular tableside preparations. The wine list showcases one of the largest private collections of Spanish wines in the world. Still, it is often the Cuban sandwich's reputation that lures customers who might be unfamiliar with those aspects of the restaurant. It is the shiny object that attracts media attention when Super Bowls or conventions come to town. *Food & Wine* magazine in 2021 named the Columbia's Cuban the Best Sandwich in Florida.

Gonzmart recognizes the sandwich's power to lure customers. He tells the story of the day when three men came in wanting Cuban sandwiches for dinner. A longtime server who had their table was upset. "We shouldn't serve them a Cuban sandwich; it's not on the dinner menu," he told Gonzmart.

"I said, 'Serve them the Cuban sandwich. You don't know who these people are,'" he remembers. "About ten minutes later, he comes up to me and says, 'They ordered a bottle of Dom Perignon!' The guys had been on their yacht and they wanted a Cuban."

As someone who cherishes the past, Gonzmart understands the passions the sandwich elicits. You start eating one as a child and you see your grandparents and great-grandparents eat it, he says. "Therefore, when you eat it, there are memories. When you eat a certain type of food, it helps you to think back to good memories. It makes it more enjoyable." Remaking the sandwich was more than a quest to make a menu item more appealing. It was an effort at time travel, to preserve what the heart says is good and happy and warm.

"These foods, to try and preserve them . . . in some cases, it's going back to the way they did it before," he said. "The Cuban sandwich, I feel that the sandwich we make is accurate to the early years. I really do."

2

Sandwiches

Pan Cubano

Since 1915, Cuban style *pan de agua* (bread made with water), known as Cuban bread, has been baked into yard-long loaves at La Segunda Central Bakery in Tampa's immigrant enclave of Ybor City. With long strips of palmetto leaf splitting the top, the loaves seem long and unruly beside a plump, uniform baguette, with its even cuts along the top. The bread is crusty, craggy even. The flaky exterior shatters with a bite, giving way to a fluffy interior. With minimal added fat, "water" bread's shelf life is typically a single day. The Cuban bread produced in Ybor City is so notorious for littering tables with crumbs and shards that local waiters began carrying scrapers to brush aside the detritus from tablecloths between courses. La Segunda's virtually unchanged product gives us a window into the evolution of Cuban bread. Here too, the Cubans of Florida are divided. Between Tampa and Miami, the approach to making Cuban bread is separated by generations and the circumstances of immigration and exile.

The Spanish believed that bread was a symbol of Western civilization—it was used in the Christian sacrament of communion, after all. As a tropical country, Cuba had never cultivated wheat but depended on imports. The scarcity of flour was a recurring cause for concern in the colony. Cubans tended to have small, simple kitchens without ovens or the desire to heat up their houses baking fresh bread. For those living in cities and towns, this was left to commercial bakeries. As early as the 1830s, visitors noted the high quality of Cuba's bread.[1]

The shape of Cuban bread is a reminder of the difficult days there. To avoid starvation, legend says, bakers literally stretched their bread into long, thin loaves, enabling hungry Cubans to cut small, conservative slices for rationing.

Journalists' accounts of the vendors in Havana confirm the change between the late 1890s and the early 1900s. Cuban bread vendors walked the streets with large wicker baskets perched on their heads, lined with a blanket and filled with loaves. Whereas Cuban bread assumed the shape of squat, round loaves before the War for Independence like "overgrown biscuits," the thin *pan de flauta* (fluted bread) became a standard type of bread afterward. In 1906, a journalist noted, "When the loaf is cut, the slices are no bigger around than our silver dollar." It is easy to see the similarities between *pan Cubano* and Spanish *barra* bread. Cubans also consumed typical sandwich bread, or *pan de molde,* also known as Pullman bread, named after the train cars that helped standardize the box-shaped loaf.[2]

Journalists in the United States tended to describe Cuban bread in superlatives. In 1899, the *New Orleans Times-Picayune,* from a city which was well-versed in excellent bread, enthused, "Cuba does have the best bread in the world." The *Minneapolis Journal* swooned in 1906, "Cuban bread is something to dream about long afterwards." In 1909, a woman writing to the *Indianapolis Star* reported, "Cuban bread, made in loaves more than a yard in length, is far superior to any made in our own land."[3]

Cuban bread inspired by that era has a characteristic strip down the length of the top. According to scholar Jono Miller, the palmetto leaf served as a temperature gauge of sorts. In the old days of uneven wood-fired ovens, if the palmetto leaf began to scorch, it served as a visual cue to the baker to rotate the loaf or shift it to a cooler part of the oven.[4]

Although Americans seemed to universally love Cuban bread at first taste, they were often puzzled by the appearance of the era's signature palmetto leaves that crowned each loaf. Some correspondents erroneously assumed that the bread was wrapped in banana leaves while baking. A *New York Times* correspondent observed,

> Cuban bread is very good. The little loaves—rolls we call them—are put in banana leaves to be baked. At the restaurants one is served with French bread. This, too, is baked in banana leaves, if I mistake not, and often little pieces of the leaves are still clinging to the loaves when they are brought to the table. They do not spoil the bread, however, as they have a clean appearance.[5]

An American housewife living in Cuba noted,

Cuban bread almost invariably is the product of the [professional] baker, and is excellent in quality. The shape of the loaf is always the same—long, narrow and flat. Sometimes the suspicious American will find at his first meal a bit of what seems to be brown paper adhering to the top of the loaf. In Cuba each baker purchases daily a certain number of green banana leaves, a strip of which is fastened to the top of each loaf, for the purpose of preventing the bread from rising too high in the heat of the oven. Certainly the result is a crisp, crusty loaf, highly pleasing alike to eye and taste.[6]

When Tampa's Cuban community began baking the distinctive fluted Cuban bread of the 1890s, long and thin, it preserved a tradition all but forgotten by those on the island today. One could argue that those long loaves ran through the entire workday, when most workers woke to a breakfast of *café con leche* and buttered Cuban bread. The morning refresher set off a succession of miniature feasts throughout the day, which concluded with dinner and the last of the bread.

Because skilled cigar workers in Havana and Tampa were "the means of production," they took breaks regularly throughout the day, seeking out snacks in nearby cafés. These breaks were later minimized by the *cafeteros,* or coffee vendors, who kept the workers well-supplied with coffee and other refreshments at their work benches. Still, workers regularly left the factories for coffee and conversation in the morning and afternoon, when snacks and sandwiches (which were often available in smaller sizes than they are today) were most popular during the work week. For all of its tasty perks, the structure of the work day restricted snacking impulses. During weekends, the cafés brimmed with coffee and conversation, and street vendors all over Cuba deployed their wares, a panoply of portable bites and delights available at virtually all hours. At night when the tropical heat receded, Cuba's nocturnal appetite emerged, when every morsel would serve to prolong the evening's pleasures or satiate them. The Cuban loaf cradled the people's most elaborate sandwich and, in the process, traced the prosperity of the exile community.[7]

The Sandwich Age

Cuba achieved independence at a time when sandwiches rose in popularity. Like baseball and democracy, the sandwich seemed modern, an opportunity to turn away from generations of heavy stews and everyday routines. As a symbol of modern life, mobility, and individuality, the sandwich took on central importance in cafés and on the street. These crusty morsels were always seen as a special treat, since "Cuban" sandwiches, like bread, were rarely prepared at home.

Although people had been eating sandwich-like creations for centuries, the invention of the modern sandwich is credited to the Englishman John Montagu, the Fourth Earl of Sandwich, in the late 1700s. An English aristocrat, it was said he enjoyed gambling so much that he would not rise from the card table for hours at a time. He reportedly called servants for thin slices of meat to be placed between slices of bread to keep his fingers and playing cards from becoming greasy. A piece of gossip seized upon by political enemies, this legend portrays the Earl in a negative light. Montagu was actually known more as a workaholic than an inveterate gambler while serving the British Empire. If anything, it would have been his working papers he did not want marred by grease.[8] Whether sandwiches existed before the Earl's innovation or not, the world now had a new name and a new image for them.

Across the Western world, commercially made bread became more widely available for urban dwellers in the 1800s. Sandwiches quickly rose in popularity due to their easy portability for workers and travelers. Railroad station vendors, dining cars, and steamship kitchens all sold sandwiches to customers on the go. Gone were the thick, greasy truncheons of old, the hard bread that doubled as a plate in old Europe, whose aristocrats reserved the softer "upper crust" for themselves. If they were lucky, a feudal estate's peasants might have received the discarded lower crust, which was typically soggy with the juices of the master's meal.[9]

The very name *sandwich,* a titled land of English nobility, referred to its status as an aristocratic snack. This made the preparation trendy among Europe's upper classes. Even the French, always protective of their language and cuisine, quickly accepted sandwiches and invented their own. At the height of the Victorian Age in the 1890s, upper-class women (and their hired help) across Europe and the United States adapted sandwiches into small, dainty, painstaking morsels reflective of the lifestyle of the rich.

With the electric bread slicer and meat slicer decades in the future, people put a premium on manageable, thinly sliced bread, meat, and cheese. When upper-class women adopted the sandwich as their own, it was in part because they were so difficult to make. First, a baker (typically a servant) would have to bake the dough in a loaf-shaped tin that resulted in bread that could be sliced into reasonably uniform squares. This bread would then be allowed to get semi-stale over a day or two so the loaf could hold up best to thin slicing. The staleness didn't matter much, as most sophisticated women would never think of serving crust on a sandwich. A new "upper crust" had been found, a slim morsel meant to titillate rather than satisfy the appetite.[10]

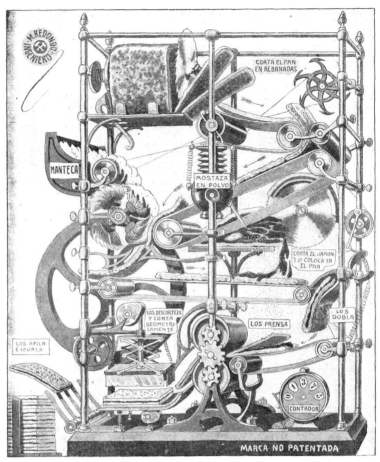

Nueva máquina modelo para fabricar *sandwiches*, sujeta a los métodos que aconseja la higiene moderna, para evitar el contacto de mano alguna, hasta que quedan en disposición,

de que el camarero los sirva al público con pu'critud y aseo.

Dib. de Redondo.

Latin America was just as smitten with sandwiches as its neighbors to the north. This elaborate sandwich-making machine dreamed up in Argentina sliced bread and applied mustard, butter, and freshly sliced ham before pressing and cutting the crusts off the sandwich. *Caras Y Caretas,* Buenos Aires, Argentina, 1914.

Carefully sliced meat was just as important to the success of a sandwich. In 1891, a newspaper in Newcastle, England, emphasized the need for thin sandwich meat, especially for English teeth.

> No housekeeper ever thought of making them of anything but sliced cold meat and people with imperfect teeth were most careful to avoid them, because the contents were scarcely ever cut small, and they were most awkward to bite. Cut up the meat, therefore, very thinly and across the grain. The sandwiches of to-day deserve to be looked upon with much greater respect. They occupy a place of honor at high-class feasts; and skillful cooks bestow the greatest pains upon them. Moreover, there are many varieties of sandwiches these days, and a skillful housekeeper never dreams of making them of "a little ham" or "a little beef" and nothing else.[11]

Soon, the Western world had seemingly tried every sandwich combination that could be fathomed. Ladies' social pages had spread recipes far and wide employing dainty nuts, dried fruit, pickled vegetables, cheeses, and pickled fish. In 1899, the *New York Sun* printed a screed on the "Modern Sandwich," including a note on all the new varieties. The writer noted that only a few years before, one would have been limited to a few types of sandwiches: ham, tongue, or corned beef, with the option of mustard. By 1899, that had radically changed. "In one big lunch establishment there are made sandwiches in 64 varieties. There would regularly be found on sale on the counter more than 20 varieties always ready."[12]

The dish resonated across society as its practical and tasty virtues became evident. For workers living in cities at the time, sandwiches simply became part of their way of life. At the Chicago World Exposition in 1893, attendees devoured one thousand pounds of ham in sandwiches each day, for some the first they had ever tasted. The sandwich had truly arrived on the world's stage.

The *Sangwich* in Cuba

Cuban anthropologist Fernando Ortiz developed the idea of "transculturation," cultural mixing and exchange in relation to Cuban culture, using the traditional stew, *ajiaco,* as an illustration. With Spanish beef, native chiles, and root vegetables associated with African slaves, the humble dish served as a bedrock of Cuban culture and cuisine. For Ortiz, Cuba's culture was best represented by the dish—common in Cuba and across the Caribbean (where it is also known as *sancocho*) because all of the ingredients retained their integrity, unlike the "melting pot" metaphor of the United States. Each element contributes its own flavors and textures to the stew while being suffused by the other ingredients.

If Ortiz's metaphor of *ajiaco* helped to explain the varied influences on colonial Cuba, perhaps no dish illustrates modern Cuba's history better than the Cuban sandwich, a dish that represents the realities of urban life, reveals the influence of other cultures, and reflects modern aspirations. At its center is the deep love for pork, which the Spanish had brought to the New World. The other components of the sandwich, such as Cuban bread, reflect the growing complexity of global economics and cuisine. In contrast to the rustic simplicity of *ajiaco,* the sandwich is complex and largely dependent on imported and/or processed ingredients, such as wheat flour, cheese, and so on. Rather than a one-pot communal experience that could theoretically simmer forever with added ingredients, the sandwich was personal, portable, public, and pricey in comparison.

The search for evidence of sandwiches in Cuba is complicated by several factors, especially because there is no fixed word in Spanish for the term that doesn't also refer to something else. Until the word *sándwich* was adopted, no single word had been used. *Bocadillo* could refer to all manner of "small bites." Sandwiches were also known as *emparedados,* a term meaning "walled or surrounded by walls."[13] The earliest known written references to sandwiches in Cuban sources are associated with imported ingredients. An 1873 Cuban newspaper ad for a lunch salon in Havana reveals that a wide variety of sandwiches were already available with imported ingredients. "Every day there are sandwiches made of turkey, lobster cooked with champagne, English sausages, Westphalian ham, venison tongue, roast beef, corned beef, etc."[14]

Another ad in 1880 for Panadería Francesa El Aguila (The Eagle French Bakery) featured imports as well.

> Do not forget the excellent and magnificent French bread of our accredited establishment, as well as a complete assortment of bakery items, such as sandwich breads, cookies of all kinds, biscuits, pastries, etc. Composed hams, from the Ferris brand, imported by the Central Refrigerator, which are the best from New York.[15]

Ted Henken, author of *Cuba: A Global Studies Handbook,* speculated that Cuba's "famed sandwiches . . . arrived with the North Americans at the turn of the nineteenth century." But this is a simplified view. Cubans were also inspired by the popularity of counterparts in Spain and elsewhere in Europe.[16]

Articles and ads about sandwiches had been appearing in Spanish newspapers and journals since the 1850s. Just as in England and the United States, sandwich vendors populated the streets of Spanish cities in the late 1800s. Ads appeared in Madrid newspapers in Spanish and French featuring a wide variety of fillings, including roast beef, salami, ham, tongue, deviled meats, preserves, and so on. Lighter creations such as the *montadito*-style (mounted) open-faced sandwich meant that people could snack twice as often.[17]

The word *bocadillo* could refer to a variety of snacks and confections, but the Spanish-style sandwich is among the most enduring. Built on slim crusty French-style bread, or *barra,* with few if any condiments, the *bocadillo* might include fish, eggs, or vegetables, but usually contained meats and their cured derivatives, such as Serrano ham, *salchichón, sobrasada,* and *pâté.* Although they could serve as a meal on the run, they were most often "small bites," as their name suggests, eaten between meals or while drinking beer, wine, or the hard cider common to much of northern Spain.[18]

It is not known when Cubans first adopted sandwiches as their own. Taking into account their obsession with food, it is safe to say that it did not take long. In 1882, Havana's El Pasaje restaurant offered a wide variety of cold cuts, including *longaniza* sausage, smoked sausage, *jamón,* bologna, smoked tongue, *salchichón, queso de puerco* (pig's head cheese), boned turkey, chicken, roast beef, and more. Ham or roast pork sandwiches became perennial favorites of Cubans.[19]

As their homeland recovered from years of scorched-earth warfare, Cubans celebrated the sandwich as a snack between meals or as feasts in themselves. In a column titled "The Sandwich and the Role It Plays in Our Great World," Cuban newspaper *El Mundo* mentioned *bocadillos, emparedados,* and *medianoches* as "successors to the sandwich," which had become an indispensable part of the Cuban menu by 1900. Newspaper articles aimed at Cuban women featured sandwiches regularly, always presenting the delicate ideal favored by the rich.[20]

In 1917, a wealthy housewife whose name appears as simply "Marjorie" sent a letter to *El Mundo* from New York City, in which she waxed poetic about the delicate creations and exclusive locations favored by her class.

Have you not noticed, my dear readers, how appetizing is the appearance of a delicately prepared sandwich? In the big New York hotels, along Fifth Avenue, in the Waldorf Astoria, the Elizabeth, and the Maillard's, where we take the five o'clock tea, we never miss an appetizing sandwich that we eat with delight, especially after a day of shopping in the stores. We rest from a few hours of fatigue and "pesquisas" [market inquiries], we take in the view, admiring the beautiful panorama of a winter afternoon, on the most chic of avenues in the metropolis, savoring an exquisite sandwich with a cup of tea.

Marjorie recognized the central place the sandwich occupied in public life and social events.

> This sandwich is a true appetizer, simple to make, and it is not expensive. At weddings, baptisms, birthday celebrations or other important events ["santos"—saint feast days], it is not possible to do without the sandwich, which we eat before the sweets, and without it there is something that we lack and we do not feel complete. The chicken, turkey, *foie gras,* and *mixto* are very appropriate for these occasions. There are some very appetizing cheese sandwiches that are made from large slices of bread, cut very fine and spread with butter and with a bit of cucumber and mustard; it can be served as is or all toasted together and eaten hot.[21]

The column in the women's section of *El Mundo* called "Sandwiches: What to Call Them and How to Make Them" described a nameless mixed sandwich. Aside from the fillings, the instructions are almost identical to those written in English decades before for high-class appetizers:

> To make sandwiches you have to start with bread expressly made for that purpose, baked in a square mold [*pan de molde*]. The bread is spread with fresh lard mixed with a bit of mustard, on two slices cut the same size, and on one of them place a slice of turkey or chicken breast, one slice of gruyere cheese, one thin slice of ham or another meat, cover with the other slice of bread, press them a bit, and cut the sides so as to make a square.[22]

If the social pages of Havana's newspapers of the period are to be believed, most Cubans took their dinners standing around fancy buffets, and the menu was always the same: dainty sandwiches, *dulces* (sweets) and *helados* (tropical ice cream), all washed down with plenty of champagne and lager. The basic menu had become so ingrained in high society that when large clubs threw parties, members created formal committees for publicity, music, ice cream, and, of course, sandwiches.[23]

In 1903, the Anón del Prado café advertised in *Diario de la Marina,* "To families: We offer you when you depart from the theater the most exquisite chocolates, excellent pure milk, rich ice creams and shortbreads, and succulent special sandwiches."[24] Havana's active nightlife required a variation, a sandwich designed for late night, the *medianoche* (midnight sandwich), a petite *mixto* served on soft, sweet, yellow-tinted egg bread. Theatergoers and late-night dancers relied on medianoches as a savory nocturnal snack. Like the stately horse-drawn coaches of Cuba's rich (soon replaced by Model Ts and later Cadillacs), evening sandwiches denoted not a humble working lunch but a hand-held extravagance, a night on the town that never had to end.

In 1921, a Cuban journalist described the central role of the sandwich in the evening:

> It's eleven at night. Many passengers ride on the coach carrying small packages with multicolored striped paper. The sandwich is an important factor in Havana life. It is the proof of a man's love for his woman, which often puts an end to the morning quarrel, or softens feminine anger by the delay in the arrival of he who is bringing home the sandwich. There is nothing else so characteristic of Havana. The sandwich here is different from other parts, bigger, more complicated. Many times it is the concrete [embodiment] of a great affection; other times, that of a meal.[25]

For common people, sandwiches were an easy way to fill up, especially when made on *pan de flauta,* which can pack a greater quantity of meat and bread into a unit of varying length. Seen as either a meal, a snack, or a love letter, the sandwich was perfectly suited to the Cuban penchant for being on the move and snacking at all hours.

The *Lonchero* and *Mixto*

A fictional serial in the *Chicago Tribune* featured a description of a *lonchero* in 1943. "A Cuban spiced ham hung from the ceiling by a rope and Juan, the counter boy, was spinning it and cutting thin slices from it with extraordinary skill, his flashing knife catching the pieces in midair and flipping them between long sections of crisp bread without for an instant interrupting the flow of conversation with his clients."[26]

Professional carvers called *loncheros* became a visible fixture around Havana and Cuba's bigger towns. The carvers often stood ensconced behind a glass enclosure at a prominent counter that faced the customers, sometimes directly facing the sidewalk outside with an open window, or *ventanita.* The best of the knife-wielding specialists made each sandwich to order and offered customers multiple fillings to choose from. By the time of independence, restaurants and cafés that advertised the presence of a *lonchero* signified the availability of expertly carved sandwiches. A column in *Diario de la Marina* is notable for the importance it attaches to *loncheros.* Two men named Pirolo had become popular in Havana, and each represented different generations of Cuban heroes, as expressed so colorfully below.

En el Lunch del Café "Europa"

¡Alto al Sandwich!

Al de éste caballero, no le ponga Vd. mostaza ni pepinos, porque está enfermo y su mal no le permite comer picantes. Cúrese amigo y entonces podrá comer cuanta mostaza quiera y también pepinos.

Curarse es fácil.

SYRGOSOL, se vende en todas las boticas bien surtidas.

DEPOSITARIOS: Sarrá, Johnson, Taquechel, González, Majó Colomer.   PROPIETARIA: Monument Chemical Co., de Londres, 15 Fish Street Hill, Monument Square, Londres.

The figure to the right was the mascot for a digestive medicine in Cuba. Here the good doctor warns the customer of a knife-wielding *lonchero* against the consumption of pickles and mustard to avoid indigestion. The habit of eating oversized sandwiches, often late into the night, might have been a better diagnosis. *Diario de la Marina*, Habana, Cuba, 1916.

One of them, that famous actor Pirolo, brother of the acclaimed Regino López who inimitably embodied the type who sings and dances rumbas and aspires to be king of the neighborhood where he lives.

The other Pirolo, the modern Pirolo, occupies the transcendental position of "lonchero" in the Centro Alemán [German Club].[27]

The lonchero serves a very useful function in every well-organized Republic, but more than anywhere else, in Havana, a city which is distinguished by its pretty women and their Fords,[28] as well as its sandwiches whose preparation has become so complicated and requires so much art and care, that a lonchero in the Vedado makes them in a special venue covered in decorative glass like that of an apothecary, the recipes on which the life or death depends.

It is necessary to see Pirolo making a sandwich to understand all the importance this has, for the variety of tastes of those who buy them and the traditions of the loncheros, it has become a difficult science.

Pirolo, with his long black hair curled and glistening by the pomade, is forming a tower of picturesque food elements that form the sandwich. But, I repeat, it is necessary to see how he handles the big knife of his profession when cutting the crisp pan de flauta, with a single cut, opens it in two, paints with mustard or butter the two halves put on the marble, in the supine position as he says, and places in them layer by layer: ham, cheese, turkey, *ensaimada* [a sort of *pâté*], trying to cover well all the space of the bread until he puts on the lid . . . he then takes a sheet of white paper in which he wraps the artistic work with the same gusto and precision that he would wrap a bouquet of flowers . . . giving it then with his bewitching hands to the customer . . . and if in course of the operation a beautiful woman passes by, Pirolo enjoys the visual feast she offers, but without stopping cutting the ham or cheese or any other of the ingredients, and— this is the most admirable of his noble labor—without his knife being diverted and cutting something more than what is entrusted to his job.

A lonchero answers the greeting of a friend who passes by . . . and like barbers, look at all the skirts passing by, yet never puts on a slice that is not warranted in his sandwiches, has the right to enter the temple of fame.[29]

Clad in the accoutrements of New York City's fashionable sandwiches at the time (mustard, pickles, and Swiss cheese) the *mixto* sandwich became trendy after Cuban independence. Because *loncheros* carved multiple meats, they could offer—or customers could request—whatever combination of ingredients they wanted. A Cuban newspaper in 1916 described a creation with "a good piece of bread wrapped in paper with ham, turkey, foie gras, cheese, butter; what in vulgar language is called an *emparedado* and in English *sandwich* or such."[30]

The Cuban love of their bread and sandwiches was on full display in 1917, when they were forced to ration flour during World War I. A front-page poem in *El Mundo* expressed the anguish brought on by the lack of bread.

With a loaf of fluted bread, let's get to work!
You, loaf of bread, I want to sing to your august memory,
sweet memory of those happy days that are gone,
in which you, divine bread, you, soft and good,
calmed the hunger that is so fierce today,
And such wonderful company you provided to
the cheese and steak and syrup, and a pair of eggs!

Oh, bread! Oh, traitor, your absence has left me with no more consolation
    than that of
the roasted sweet potato when I have it!
Where have you run away to? I have not seen you for a long time;
I have been hungry and dizzy for a long time.
Without you, even though I eat, I never get full
Bread of my life, how I love you; how I look for you; how I long for you;
for you I sigh, with you I dream, and although I'm so anxious, I never find you!
If only I could, my bread, see you again, to bite your beak with rapture;
to dip in sauce and fresh eggs; to eat on a sandwich, alone or with cheese . . .
Sweet memory of those happy days that are gone![31]

Mixto as Export

The sandwich is a relatively recent addition to the Cuban culinary pantheon. No one considers it a foundational *criollo* dish but a modern novelty that was urban in nature, dependent on fresh commercially baked bread and a variety of meats, including refrigerated imports. It is impossible to tell exactly when or how the *mixto* sandwich became one of Cuba's signature exports, as it was created and popularized during a period of fluid movement between Cuba and the United States. The steamship allowed emigrants to treat exile enclaves like extensions of Cuba itself. It is there, in the oscillation of Cubans between the homeland they inherited and the one they invented abroad, where we can identify if not the origins of the Cuban sandwich, then the era and landscape in which it flourished.

An old fable that may contain a grain of truth says that Cubans largely favored *lechón* sandwiches, while *Yanquis* habitually ordered ham. Virtually every *lonchero* in Cuba kept ham and roast pork on hand. It was only a matter of time until an indulgent customer or enterprising *lonchero* first combined the two and experimented with new additions.

In a sense, it hardly matters where the first was made. Although common wisdom would have the sandwich coming from Cuba, it is also possible that a *lonchero* first stacked meats together in New York City, Tampa, or Key West. That same *lonchero* or a pleased customer could have boarded a steamship and in hours arrived at one of the other Cuban enclaves and spread word of the new delicious combination.

Although a significant Cuban population resided in Key West, especially after the first war in 1868, there is no known written evidence to support that a *lonchero* or *mixto* existed on the island any earlier than in Tampa. Historian Loy

Glenn Westfall has posited that "the Cuban sandwich was born in Havana and educated in Key West." While it is all but certain that some form of Cuban sandwich was consumed in Key West, Tampa and New York City before 1900, there are no known documents to prove it or describe it.

The appearance of the *mixto* immediately seized the imaginations and appetites of *Yanquis*. The sandwich's bread and strata of ingredients made it more memorable and indulgent than its counterparts at the time. Based upon this appeal, the "Cuban sandwich" became a sensation in the United States but much was lost in translation. When prepared outside Cuban enclaves, the sandwich was more of a concept than a recipe, and often bore little resemblance to anything eaten by the Cubans themselves.

The earliest known reference to any "Cuban sandwich" in the United States is in a military joke. Cuba apparently already had a reputation for sandwiches in 1898. When soldiers found little to eat on the island, they created what became mockingly known as "Cuban sandwiches" from the only palatable morsels in their rations. A writer for the *Missoulian News* in Montana wrote, "The Cuban sandwich, two hardtack [a hard biscuit or cracker] and a bean, are not served at the pink teas and other functions even by the most patriotic American women."[32]

By 1900, Cuban sandwiches of a different kind were a new sensation in New York City, home to one of the oldest Cuban communities in the United States.[33] For most Americans, the allure of a Cuban sandwich was its layers of ingredients. Several newspapers printed detailed descriptions of a crustless creation.

A sandwich which is popular at Cuban restaurants and has acquired the name of Cuban bears a close resemblance to the familiar club sandwich. It is made with two thin slices of ordinary wheat loaf made in sandwich form. No butter is used, but on the lower side is placed, first, a layer of the breast of cold chicken cut very thin; over this goes more wafer-thin slices of cold boiled ham, the cucumber pickles also sliced very thin: shavings of bologna sausage top the pickle, and over the sausage slices of cheese. The bread top is then put on and the whole is fitted into an oblong frame which neatly and quickly trims off the crust and shapes the sandwich. It is then folded in plain white paper and delivered, the whole operation having been accomplished in sight of the purchaser and in an incredibly short space of time. Twenty cents of our money pays for the sandwich, which is eaten with a glass of wine or of beer.[34]

Here we find the Cuban sandwich cradled not by a section of Cuban loaf but by sliced bread. The club sandwich (turkey, bacon, lettuce, tomato, and mayonnaise on three layers of toasted bread, sometimes with ham), which is said to date back to 1889 in New York, rose to prominence because it was both delicate and indulgent. It is no surprise that when most Americans encountered the *mixto* or Cuban sandwich, the club sandwich was the closest comparable thing, except the Cuban did not employ a third slice of bread in the middle, and would later be distinctive for being served on sections of fluted Cuban or French bread. Is it a coincidence that the first known descriptions of "Cuban sandwiches" are from the same city that produced the layered club sandwich?

Journalists described the Cuban sandwich as so large it had to be eaten with a knife and fork. In 1901, the *New York Tribune* wrote, "Cuban sandwiches are considered by many an improvement on the popular club variety, and, like them, they are put together in different strata. Thin buttered slices of white or brown bread are used," with a slice of chicken or turkey, pickles, bologna, and Swiss cheese. While some today may scoff at the presence of bologna in their sandwiches, the journalist might have been referring to mortadella, an old favorite on the island that is still popular among exiles and occasionally appears in mixed sandwiches.[35]

In addition to pies, pastries, sweet cakes, and tropical ices, a journalist in Cuba pointed out the sandwiches she saw in 1903. Her evocative description is worth quoting at length.

> Havana is a city of cafes. There are hundreds of them, of all classes, in all parts of town. It is strange, indeed, if one passes a block without seeing one or more. At all times of the day there are men sitting at the tables. At breakfast time, 11 o'clock, there are so many men seated there that one wonders if any of the heads of families eat at home. Buckets carry the working man's meals to him or are taken by him, and often entire families have their meals brought in this way from neighboring restaurants. One unused to "cantinas" is apt to wonder why so many men go about the streets carrying milk pails. A tiny charcoal burner is sometimes placed in the lowest of the several compartments, and in this way the dinner may be kept warm. On the counters of the restaurants are all kinds of baked meats and fowl. The hams are all spiced.
>
> Sandwiches are piled up high, but they are not the kind we know, that is a simple layer of meat, or nuts, or lettuce. The Cuban sandwich is made of a roll, and has three or four things between the sides. The kind known as *medianoche,* suggesting that it is usually eaten late at night, is of a very delicious roll, with chicken and bits of pickle between the sides. Ham, cheese and pickle are the ordinary filling for a native sandwich.[36]

A journalist in South Carolina left Cuba enthused by his discovery,

> We sampled some of the remarkable Cuban sandwiches. First comes a layer of ham, then sausage, turkey, pickle, mustard and Swiss cheese, all evenly distributed and tightly pressed between the layers of bread. The largest mouth in our party could not attempt to bite through one of these three story structures; so we were feign to content ourselves with dissecting the layers and studying their anatomy, story by story.[37]

In 1913, ads in Tennessee reported on "the new rage that's sweeping Florida." By the end of the 1920s, the Cuban sandwich had caught on all around the Sunshine State: St. Petersburg, Orlando, Fort Myers, Miami, Key West, and Tallahassee businesses all ran ads naming the sandwich as a specialty. From the 1890s until the 1950s, Tampa was home to the largest Cuban enclave in the United States and a proud promoter of the Cuban sandwich.[38]

Claudio Rodríguez, Morrison Meat Packers (Miami)

It's important that the Cuban sandwich be well stacked with meat, according to the Rodríguez family. Pale pink and a little sweet, bolo hams form the basis for the filling of most Cuban sandwiches. The name is derived from the shape of the ham, which is deboned and pressed into a round "ball" shape for easy handling and slicing. This is the type of ham José Rodríguez, a *guajiro* (rural farmer) from the Cuban countryside in Pinar del Río, knew when he immigrated to the United States in 1957.

First settling in New Orleans, José found work at the distribution center for Morrison's Cafeteria. There, he cut steaks, ground beef, and prepared other meat for a few years before being lured to Miami at the invitation of a friend, Pancho Bulnes. When they started their own meat-packing business, José proposed they give it an Anglo name as a nod to his first employer in the United States. Thus, Morrison Meat Provisions was born—an American-sounding name, but proudly featuring Cuban-style products.

After enjoying success with the business, José was involved in a serious auto accident, sustaining life-threatening injuries. He spent the next year in and out of the hospital, slowly recuperating and eventually returning to work. José's son Claudio remembers: "My dad was not one hundred percent when he tried

Among its line of meat products, Morrison Meat Packers produces boneless bolo hams, a style that is very popular for use in Cuban sandwiches. Courtesy Morrison Meat Packers.

to come back to the business. Pancho invited him to set up shop on the second floor of his two-story plant, and the two partners split. Pancho also offered José lesser cuts of meat that he couldn't sell (like the bottom round, which was tougher); from these José started his new business by making *tasajo* [Cuban beef jerky.]" That was the beginning of Morrison Meat Packers.

As a young man, Claudio Rodríguez had no intention of going into the family business despite having spent his childhood at his father José's meat processing plant. When asked if he had fond memories of growing up in his father's factory, Claudio replies: "Truthfully, no. I would be picked up from school and go to the plant, make hams, and do whatever needed to be done. But I had no intentions of going into this business. I wanted to be an architect."

Although Claudio had received some scholarships to go out of state and pursue his dream of being an architect, as he was getting ready to leave Miami, he felt the pressure from his family to stay home given his father's health. Claudio decided to study architecture at the local community college and continued to work in the family business. Later, on the advice of a college professor, Claudio changed his major to business and took over the operations at Morrison Meat Packers.

Some things have stayed the same as in the old days: they still buy whole, fresh hams from North Carolina, prepare them in the sweet Cuban style, and provision a number of grocery stores, bakeries, and restaurants. Claudio's son, Kevin, has joined the family business, too—despite having fulfilled his father's dream of going out of state to study architecture. When Kevin returned to Miami, he grew disenchanted with his new field and eventually returned to the family fold, just as his father had done a generation earlier.

Today Morrison Meat Packers is the largest supplier of Cuban-style hams in the United States. They are also purveyors of *pierna prensada* (cooked seasoned pork), *lacón* (a variety of ham from the Galicia region in Northern Spain), and other specialty Spanish hams, with distribution throughout the Southeastern United States, the Northeast, and Central and South America. Although the Cuban sandwich has several components, Claudio believes the meat quality is all-important. As the family looks to the future for new opportunities and products—Italian sausages and diced ham are two additions to their traditional offerings—it is clear that the passion and tradition of family and culture will continue to drive the business and fill sandwiches.

Morrison Meat Packers is run by its founding family. *From left to right*: Claudio, Gilda, Kevin, and Danny. The company grew from humble beginnings to satisfy the appetites of a generation of fellow exiles. Courtesy Morrison Meat Packers.

Nicole Valls, Versailles Restaurant (Miami)

Growing up in Miami, Nicole Valls' earliest memories involve the Cuban sandwich.

Whenever her father, Felipe Valls Jr., would come home late from work, he'd bring the family Cuban sandwiches, tropical mamey shakes, and other Cuban pastries and goodies.

"Whenever we'd go to the beach or on the boat, we would pass by Versailles and get a bunch of Cuban Sandwiches and eat them throughout the day."

It made sense, since her father worked with her grandfather, Felipe Valls Sr., founder of Versailles Cuban Restaurant, where Miami locals pronounce it "Ver-sah-yes." Now grown, Nicole helps operate Miami's most famous Cuban restaurant, with its mirror-walled dining rooms (hence the name), bakery and *ventanita* ("little window") coffee window for walk-up sandwiches, cafecitos, and pastries.

Nestled in the heart of Little Havana since 1971, the family operation grew from one location on Calle Ocho into a restaurant empire that now includes dozens of locations, including Versailles's sister Cuban restaurant across Calle Ocho, La Carreta, Mesa Mar Seafood Table in Coral Gables, and Manchu Wok sushi restaurants in Miami International Airport. Several mini-versions of Versailles and La Carreta operate at the airport and Hard Rock Stadium as well.

Soon after the flagship opened, Versailles became a de facto town square for expatriate Cuban-Americans to gather at the restaurant's coffee windows and argue politics. Whenever an election loomed, a political debate erupted, or a local sports team won a championship, Versailles was ground zero for collective outpourings of emotion: joyous celebrations, loud protests, and solemn mournings.

When Cuban dictator Fidel Castro died in November 2016, Versailles became the place to vent about his fifty-year purge of their homeland. The resulting explosion of emotion had been anticipated for years. For a decade before Castro's death, Valls kept a folder in the trunk of her car with a playbook for how the restaurant would react in that event. She immediately texted the managers to clear the parking lot so that news vans with satellite dishes could park for remote reports from the heart of the rage. Crowds surrounded Versailles, chanting rhythmically in Spanish while banging pots and pans.

That kind of magnetism has made Versailles a landmark for more than its food alone. When actor, writer, and director Jon Favreau wrote the screenplay for his 2014 film *Chef*, in which the sandwich was practically featured as costar, he could not resist filming at Versailles.

"[I thought] how great it would be to go to Versailles and try a Cubano," Favreau told the *Miami New Times* in 2014. From that moment, Favreau's down-on-his-luck character gets the inspiration to make Cuban sandwiches the centerpiece of his food truck's cuisine, and the cornerstone to rebuilding his career. To accommodate that scene, management had to close half of the restaurant on a busy Saturday night and have a hundred Cuban sandwiches ready to go for actors to eat on camera.

"They were here for a full day and we're in it briefly," Valls said. "It's crazy how long those scenes take." Such is the burden of being an icon. To meet that burden, the company operates a central processing plant where they receive ingredients for the menus of the various restaurants, including the proteins used on the Cuban sandwich that are butchered in-house and then shipped to locations.

Having a commissary ensures consistency and quality of ingredients. "We're not leaving it up to the managers," Valls says. "They're not going to buy some-

Versailles Restaurant and its *ventanita* (service window) have become the epicenter of Cuban life in Miami. Founder Felipe Valls, *center,* poses with his son, Felipe Jr., and granddaughter Nicole outside the iconic eatery in Miami. Courtesy of Versailles Cuban Restaurant.

thing that's cheaper to lower their food costs. No. This is our spec [specification]. This is what you're getting. You don't have them ordering from a hundred different places and receiving deliveries from a hundred trucks. Everything comes from our plant and from our bakery."

The Versailles bakery makes bread for all locations, but the company must supplement with Cuban bread baked from vendors to their specifications. "It's getting harder and harder to find places that make good, authentic Cuban bread," she says.

Café con leche and croquetas are ubiquitous at the ventanita, but inside the self-trademarked "World's Most Famous Cuban Restaurant," the most popular entree is the Churrasco Versailles skirt steak served with *moros* rice (a mixture of rice with black beans), sweet fried plantains, and chimichurri sauce. The Cuban is the most popular sandwich, far outpacing the *pan con bistec* (steak sandwich).

Each Cuban sandwich starts off as a yard-long loaf of pan Cubano. With the ends squared off and the loaf split lengthwise, the top slice of bread is buttered lightly on the interior crumb. The bottom slice starts with one pound of sliced sweet ham layered end to end, followed by another layer of ten ounces of roast pork sliced into medallions. Ten ounces of sliced Swiss cheese lay on top, then covered with the buttered loaf.

Once assembled, it's either sliced in quarters for "Our Famous Cuban" or in foot-long thirds for a larger "Special Cuban." The individual portions are taken to a press, where the sandwich is opened between the ham and pork layers and laid face down on the hot *plancha* in order to heat the proteins and melt the cheese more efficiently over the pork. Pressing the interior of the sandwich ensures that it is always heated through properly, with the kiss of the griddle enhancing the flavors of the meat. A slathering of butter is applied to the exterior of the bread before the lid of the press is closed. After six to seven minutes in the press, both halves are flipped onto their bread. One half gets a drizzle of mustard over the now-griddled ham layer followed by two thinly sliced dill pickle chips. The sandwich is then assembled into one piece and pressed for another two to three minutes. After it finishes, the sandwich is sliced corner to corner on a diagonal bias at a 10-degree angle.

In a community that can passionately disagree about all manner of cooking questions, the Valls family managed to make Versailles and La Carreta landmarks for tourists and locals alike. In the process, the Valls family has played the role of tastemakers for the exile community in every sense: creating a new exile identity for Miami's Cuban exiles at the dinner table, the *ventanita,* and beyond.

3

Cigar Cities

Born in Valencia, Spain, in 1818, Vicente Martínez Ybor became a cigar magnate in Havana as a young man with successful premium brands such as Príncipe de Gales (Prince of Wales). Ybor's factories specialized in producing hand-rolled cigars using the finest "clear Havana" tobacco, considered the best in the world. Although he was born a Spaniard, Ybor sympathized with the cause of Cuban independence from Spain. When Cuban rebels took up arms against the Spanish in 1868, Ybor's pro-Cuba political leanings forced him to flee for his life. Virtually overnight, he too had become an exile of sorts.

Along with the Cuban insurrection, a high US tariff on finished cigars persuaded many producers such as Ybor to relocate their operations to the United States. In the 1860s and 1870s, Cuban labor and tobacco made Key West a center of cigar production that almost rivalled old Havana. While Key West functioned as an expedient solution, it was not an ideal permanent home. The cigar industry was poised for growth, but its improvised island home was isolated, small, and lacked a robust water supply. Cigar producers had also grown weary of chronic labor unrest, especially when confined in such a small space.

The small Florida town of Tampa joined Galveston, Mobile, and Pensacola in trying to draw Ybor's factories to their locales. Tampa's Board of Trade sweetened the deal sufficiently for Ybor to buy property, and his friend and colleague, cigar producer Ignacio Haya, followed suit. The biggest challenge Tampa presented to the industry was the lack of specialized workers, which would have to be imported from Cuba and Key West. Years of unrest in Cuba and exile abroad had forged a remarkably mobile workforce.

Ybor planned a new town built around cigar factories in the scrubby, sandy wilds of Florida, a project that attracted an eager workforce with offers of well-paying positions in factories with plenty of work. With a low cost of living compared to Havana, Tampa offered immigrant workers a chance to get ahead. Most of the newcomers probably had no intention of staying for long. A fire in Key West gutted several cigar factories in 1886, the year after Ybor City was founded about 240 miles to the north. Cuba's offshore cigar industry gave the sleepy scrub town of Tampa a shot of economic and cultural vitality.

The hand-rolled cigar industry relied on a workforce of skilled immigrants comprised mostly of Cubans soon to be joined by growing minorities of Spanish and Sicilian newcomers. Men and women, black and white, often worked side by side in Florida's cigar factories, a rare sight, especially in the Deep South. In the ethnic enclaves of Ybor City and West Tampa, the racial Jim Crow line pervasive across the South blurred with the presence of so many "Latins" and Afro-Cubans of often indistinguishable racial lineage. Tensions between militant labor unions and reactionary manufacturers meant strikes and factory lockouts occurred regularly.

The newcomers built an immigrant world with a bustling economy and vibrant blend of cultures. Cubans had become adept at quickly organizing similar enclaves around the hemisphere. Along with their unions and social clubs, the immigrants quickly developed theaters, newspapers, and restaurants. Most of all, they specialized in casual cafés like those found in Havana, offering simple menus built around Cuban bread, *café con leche,* and snacks such as the Cuban sandwich. Tampa's new profusion of restaurants and cafés could soon count on local bakeries and coffee mills. Thus supplied, Cuban entrepreneurs attempted to duplicate their customers' old lifestyles in a new land.

A Tampa journalist observed the same workday routines practiced in Havana.

One of the unique features in force among the many of the factories of Tampa is the coffee hour. Many of the work men do not take breakfast before starting to work. They work until well along in the morning, then "knock off" for a while and go out to a coffee shop for the morning refreshment, which may include a Cuban sandwich, coffee, or other items. This break in the morning's labor refreshes the workers, makes them feel better and improves the quality and quantity of the work.[1]

Over time, Tampa's business class marketed its "Latin" culture as an asset. City leaders had already demonstrated their desire to run a "wide open" town with gambling and illicit nightlife spiced up by *bolita,* a popular but illegal lottery inspired by the Cuban *lotería.* Beyond cigars and vice, Tampa's city boosters offered Cuban bread, Spanish Bean Soup, Cuban sandwiches, *arroz con pollo,* and other foods as part of Tampa's brand. *Americanos* from Tampa and beyond enjoyed visiting the Latin enclaves of Ybor City and West Tampa as if they were tourists embarking for Cuba. In 1906, a party of young socialites "enjoyed a tally ho ride" around town, enjoying "a delicious lunch of Cuban sandwiches, ice cream and cakes."[2]

In 1916, H. H. Bertrand and his wife were not very impressed with their visit to Tampa. An unusually rainy December kept them confined indoors for much of their visit. What they saw of the outdoors they didn't like much, either. Perhaps the only impressive thing they found was the "combination Cuban sandwich. It was fearfully and wonderfully made. Half a loaf of hard-crusted bread, split lengthwise, a layer of turkey, another of ham, another of sausage and still another of cheese and pickles—the whole doped with Creole sauce."[3]

Tampa residents, regardless of class or ethnicity, quickly fell in love with the sandwich. While in basic training in 1916, the only thing Carl Epping wanted more than to fight Pancho Villa (who had been known to raid across the border during the Mexican revolution) was a Cuban sandwich from his hometown of Tampa. When the new power plant in Hyde Park hosted dignitaries for an open house in 1918, Manuel García, impresario of the Grand Orient restaurant, provided Cuban sandwiches for the occasion.[4] A correspondent reveled in an international feast as he walked the streets of Ybor City. "I eat sparingly of Italian

In Havana, the sandwich was favored by the wealthy while taking carriage rides in the cool of the evening. As suggested by this 1920 ad, the same ritual played out on the streets of Tampa, Florida, with the added innovations of the Model T car and curb service. *Tampa Tribune*, 1920.

spaghetti—only one heaping dish—and drink a cup of Spanish coffee. Then to finish the repast I consume a Cuban sandwich. Passing a drink stand I imbibe a glass of genuine American [sugar] cane juice, which completed my cosmopolitan luncheon."[5]

Few situations could encapsulate old Tampa's mix of shadiness and industriousness better than the following scene in "an old restaurant in Ybor City, the time midnight. In the one corner an old player piano rattled off music—a score of Spaniards, both male and female, were joking, talking and gambling at one table, [while] twenty-eight local Tampa Eagle Scouts were furiously attempting to devour the Cuban sandwich" as part of their pledge trials.[6]

In 1927, the unfortunately named "Cho-Cho,"[7] the "famous health clown," gave lectures to Tampa's children on the benefits of nutrition. The clown paid special attention to the city's presumably less-educated Latin population. His presentation was met with delight by the youngsters until he told them not to eat pickles. Cho-Cho and most home economists at the time did not think children could digest pickles well, but his audience begged to differ. "There was just one difficulty," the *Tribune* wrote, "the pickle is an integral part of the Cuban sandwich and Ybor City kids like these typical tidbits of their race" and had been eating them for their entire lives.[8]

In 1929, Tampa's journalists began claiming the Cuban as a distinctive product. "Tampa has something that Atlanta hasn't got, and of which Atlanta might well be envious—the lowly Cuban mixed sandwich served any minute of the day or night in downtown, Ybor City and West Tampa coffee shops, cafes, and drink stands." A sandwich fan in Atlanta had "two fat 'Cuban mixed' sandwiches" sent from Tampa via air mail. In 1930, even Tampa's W. T. Grant department store's lunch counter advertised a sale on its Cuban sandwich for ten cents.[9]

When S. Monroe Staats took a driving tour of Florida in 1936, he stayed in Miami but notably only ate Cuban sandwiches when in Tampa. A tour of the state by the *New York Times* featured the cafés and Cuban sandwiches of Tampa.[10]

Tinkering with the Formula

Tampa became known for augmenting its sandwiches with yet another meat product, a thin slice of salami or *salchichón,* a hard, dry sausage often referred to as "Spanish salami" that added an extra kick of salt and fat. Enrique Fernández wistfully remembered the snacks of his youth in Old Havana, which contained more than the requisite ham and pork. When his family moved to Tampa in the 1950s, he recognized the same flavors as his favorites in Cuba.

Take a Cuban staple, the "mixed" sandwich, which I would learn to call a Cuban sandwich in Florida. There are a couple of places in the Old Havana of my childhood where it is the best. These are Spanish emporia specializing in the *jamones* and chorizos of the Old Country, as well as Spanish and Italian wines. I remember tasting ham and something tangier, chorizo, perhaps, or *sobrasada,* a Spanish cold cut similar to its Italian cognate, *sopressata.*

When we moved to Tampa we encountered the Cuban sandwich in its home turf. The Tampa version includes either salami or mortadella or both, and if my memory of Havana's *sandwiche mixto* is correct, that would be close to the Cuban original, which I recall having some similar meats added to the mix.[11]

Fernández provides evidence of other cured meats being added, along with an important connection to Tampa's devotion to salami. The popular belief that Tampa's Italians somehow introduced salami to the sandwich in the spirit of camaraderie is understandable and romantic, but probably misguided. In Cuba itself, vendors competed for customers by adding their own flair to their products. A variety of cold cuts were used to add distinctive flavors while giving customers more for their money. In Cuba and Tampa, thin slices of *salchichón,* hard chorizo, or hard salami were common but not universal. There was also the now-forgotten layer of poultry that appeared in many early accounts of Cuban sandwiches. As strange as these ingredients may seem today, they were not aberrations from a prescribed recipe but a tried and popular part of the *mixto.*

In 1937, the *Tampa Tribune* bragged,

> A mention of food in Ybor City, Tampa's Latin colony, brings Spanish bean soup and Cuban sandwiches immediately to mind. The famous Cuban sandwich is best known as a ten-inch slice of Cuban bread filled with cold ham, pork, pickle, cheese, lettuce, salami, chicken on special occasions and sometimes sliced olives. This is a typical ham and egg dish to the Cubans.[12]

Over time, the variable *mixto* became something more specific in Tampa. In 1933, the *Tribune* printed a detailed description of a locally made sandwich:

> Cubans have adopted many of the Spanish methods of cooking but have perfected a sandwich that is unusually popular in Ybor City. It is made of hard Cuban bread with a filler of turkey, pork, ham, salami, cheese, pickles, mustard, and sometimes other meats. It is served with Cuban coffee, which is made strong by being roasted until it burns. Usually the coffee is served without cream and only a small amount of sugar with a pinch of salt.[13]

In 1934, the *Ithaca Journal* in New York described the same sandwich but withheld the turkey.[14]

The *Tampa Tribune,* which was not friendly toward organized labor, had long made it a specialty to portray striking workers as lazy and overfed. In 1937, when seamstresses in Ybor City went on strike to protest inferior pay at the Works Progress Administration, the paper returned to its old mantra. "At least the makers of Cuban sandwiches are reaping a harvest of business out of the WPA women workers' sit-down strike in the Ybor City sewing center. Cuban sandwiches are the mainstay of the strikers' rations and also of the curious crowds who sit down along the sidewalks near the center. The ice cream pushcart peddlers and peanut vendors are not doing bad either. Their wares are much in demand round the strike zone."[15]

World War II had a profound effect on Florida, ushering in an unprecedented era of growth, tourism, and development. With its port, ship building facilities, and air bases, Tampa teemed with wartime activity. The massive stream of people who worked or served around Tampa often experienced Cuban cuisine for the first time. Most Americans found the Cuban sandwich to be the most approachable item on local menus.

In 1950, the *Miami Herald* highly recommended a Cuban sandwich not in Miami but in Havana. In Cuba, the delicacy was known as *surtido de flauta,* or fluted assortment. "This is a mouth-watering concoction of hard, crusty Cuban bread, cheese, ham, turkey, roast pork, and Spanish salami." Here, at long last, was Tampa's sister sandwich in Cuba, with *salchichón* and *pavo asado,* or roast turkey.[16]

Lost in Translation

As the sandwich traveled farther away from the straits of Cuba, it was often stuffed beyond recognition with all manner of unexpected ingredients. Some of the earliest recipes for the sandwich written in English are the most perplexing. One recipe the newspapers passed around between 1910 and 1920 doesn't even call for meat. "Cut two slices of bread for each person to be served. On half of the slices lay lettuce leaves spread with mayonnaise dressing. In the lettuce lay thick slices of soft cheese, cover with the remaining slices of bread and on the top layer a piece of sour dill pickle." *McClure's* syndicated menu in 1919 called for a lunch of baked bean soup, Cuban sandwiches, and canned fruit. "This sandwich is usually made so large that it is necessary to eat it with a knife and fork and may be proportioned in such a way as to supply a large amount of nourishment. Between two slices lay first lettuce with a little salad dressing or salt on it then a slice of soft mild cheese, and finally thin slices of dill pickle or a little chopped pickle." One can only wonder why anyone would make such a large sandwich out of so little.[17]

Liberally translated versions of the Cuban sandwich had been adopted and mashed up with local tastes across the United States. The concept and form of a mixed Cuban sandwich—with slices of various meats, cheese, and other ingredients—was more important to early practitioners than its typical ingredients. Journalists sacrificed accuracy for enthusiasm and publicized a panoply of creations that were more mixed than Cuban. The *Oakland Tribune* called for sliced wheat bread, butter, lettuce, mustard, pickles, and a slice of "Spanish Loaf" lunchmeat. Many bastardizations in the Midwest called for *Braunschweiger,* or liverwurst sausage *pâté*.[18] According to Joseph Erwin of the Health Kitchen at Mansfield, Ohio, in 1942, the Cuban sandwich is composed of ham, cheese, Braunschweiger, lettuce, salami, salad dressing, and more. "The whole thing is served between two pieces of Cuban or French bread cut lengthwise and as Erwin says, makes a meal in itself."[19]

The *Boston Globe*'s specimen is a liberal interpretation, suggesting rye or white bread. "Put on lettuce leaves, then slice of ham, over which a thin slice of cheese is laid, then ham over cheese, lettuce, then top crust. Mixed pickles, diced, with mayonnaise and spread between ham and cheese. Any kind of cheese is used, such as American, Swiss, Roquefort or pimento."[20]

In the 1950s, toasting sandwiches in the oven became popular among food editors. Several Cuban sandwich "melt" recipes appeared across the Midwest during the 1950s, calling for roast beef and other lunchmeats to be baked with cheddar on a hard roll. The *New York Age's* recipe called for ham, salami, and cheddar, served on hard rolls heavily slathered with a mixture of margarine and mustard. A Pennsylvania journalist used the terms Cuban sandwich and Po' Boys interchangeably, suggesting processed cheese, horseradish, onions, and olives on French bread. Another unlikely recipe called for a triple-decker of roast beef, boiled ham, and cooked lamb on French bread. These inconsistent variations on the sandwich quickly faded from the scene, but toasted sandwiches did not.[21]

The gourmand James Beard once wrote a tribute to the *medianoche* sandwich in 1971.

> I love it because I love roast pork, especially the Cuban and Puerto Rican version. You take a long sort of hero-shaped soft roll, split and butter it and put on the lower half a good portion of nicely seasoned cold roast pork

Because roughly half of Cubans would have been considered black in the United States, many would not have been able to dine in whites-only establishments in the segregated south. *Thomasville Times-Enterprise*, 1958.

and on top of that an equally healthy portion of a cheese that melts well, such as Swiss cheese, Emmental or Gruyere[.] Slap on the top of the roll and put the whole thing in the oven or on a griddle with a weight on the top so the cheese melts all over the pork. This takes its place alongside the poor boy and the hero and all those other honest party sandwiches that are so satisfying.[22]

Even the venerated gourmand James Beard just couldn't get the sandwich right when he left ham off of the *medianoche* and didn't even mention the sweet egg bread that usually cradles such a sandwich.

Sandwiches sometimes became a source of anxiety rather than comfort. In Florida, the supposed bastion of the Cuban sandwich in the United States, the sandwich had quickly become cheapened by the *Yanqui* embrace. For every passionate practitioner of the sandwich, a hundred more had appropriated cheap imitations to cash in. In the 1920s and 1930s, lunch counters in drug and department stores began serving the Cuban sandwich as a matter of routine with whatever ingredients they already had access to.

Operating on razor-thin profit margins, sandwich slingers often tried to stretch their inventory. In the summer of 1929, after weeks of food-borne illnesses plagued Tampa, the City Council urgently passed new sandwich regulations. One woman died after ingesting a sandwich at Sulphur Springs. "Only one complaint of this illness, which was traced to soft drink counter sandwiches, has been received since the regulation went into effect. The wrappers must bear the date on which the sandwich was made and no sandwich over three days old is permitted to be sold."[23]

In 1957, the Tampa Tarpons baseball team suffered when their second baseman Eddie Miller had to be rushed to the hospital in the middle of a game due to food poisoning. Cuban sandwiches made by Ace Canteen Service, which was based in Tampa, sickened at least fifty more people across seven counties and killed one. Over the years, large "canteen" companies began mass-producing sandwiches for sale by vendors, stores, lunch trucks, and gas stations. Ace and its spoiled meat represented the worst fears of people everywhere who relied on those convenient but questionable morsels. At the time, Hillsborough County only had seven health inspectors to cover 2,700 food establishments for about 350,000 residents. The county offered such low wages for inspectors that no qualified candidate wanted the six new positions created after the crisis.[24]

A Star Is Born

Tampa never settled on an exact formula, but everyone knew what to order. With or without salami and turkey (and/or the requisite *Yanqui* additions of lettuce, tomato, and mayo), served cold or pressed hot, for Tampa's "Latins" and "Anglos" alike, the Cuban sandwich had become a hometown icon. Its virtues of flavor and mobility became apparent to many during World War II, when Tampa was flush with hungry workers, soldiers, and sailors on the move. Despite high sandwich sales, people in Tampa felt the pinch during wartime rationing.

Arroz con pollo is not the only Spanish food victim [of rationing]. Those famous Cuban sandwiches too, served by thousands in Tampa everyday, contain not one, but three kinds of meat—ham, pork, and salami—in addition to all the other ingredients and they will be ruled out on meatless Tuesdays. But since turkey no longer finds its way into Cuban sandwiches as it once did, Cuban sandwiches will be eligible for serving on poultryless Thursdays.[25]

With daily Cuban sandwich sales at four hundred to seven hundred daily, the Columbia Restaurant rose to new heights of popularity during World War II. Sales spiked to seven hundred on Sundays because so many Latin families procured sandwiches for promenades, picnics, and beach outings. The Columbia claimed to sell 175,000 Cuban sandwiches a year in the early 1950s, constructed from 42,000 pounds of ham, 15,000 pounds of roast pork, 5,000 pounds of salami, 8,000 pounds of cheese, 200 gallons of mustard, 350 gallons of pickles, and 150 pounds of butter. Only five gallons of mayonnaise were used because so few people asked for it. After holidays such as Thanksgiving and Christmas, the Columbia augmented its sandwiches with slices of leftover turkey.[26]

The Cuban sandwich became Tampa's culinary brand for the humble and well-heeled alike. Musician and comedian Victor Borge delighted crowds at Tampa's Municipal Auditorium in 1946 when he munched on a Cuban sandwich while the orchestra played "Holiday for Strings."[27] Locally raised songstress Frances Langford returned to Tampa from endless touring with the United Services Organization (USO) and Bob Hope during and after the war. Fellow entertainer Patty Thomas joined her for Cuban sandwiches in Ybor City, each of them downing two apiece. "They just don't make Cuban sandwiches anywhere else in the country like they do here," she said. Seemingly, every meeting and fundraiser for political rallies, clubs, schools, and churches was furnished with Cuban sandwiches.[28]

The popularity of the Cuban sandwich inspired a new generation of artisans after World War II. In 1947, a Tampa sandwich icon was born when Angelo Cacciatore bought a humble sandwich spot called the Silver Ring in Ybor City. It had previously been a bar and then a sandwich shop. Cacciatore opened with a menu devoted to hamburgers but soon changed to thirty-five-cent Cuban sandwiches. Other than the sandwich, the Silver Ring specialized in *bolita* sales and an occasional game of poker in the back.

After work one night, Angelo and his brother Frank walked to the Sons of Sicily Hall behind the restaurant on Eighth Avenue. There they watched a poker game in progress when one of the players ordered half a dozen sandwiches to be delivered from the Silver Ring. Angelo sighed that he was tired after a long day, but the gambler flung a twenty-dollar bill on the table. At the time, Angelo's daily take was twenty or thirty dollars, so he jumped at the chance and returned to the Silver Ring.

Cacciatore piled the extra-large sandwiches high with double meat and cheese for the high-paying customer. The *Cubanos* were a big hit among the card players, and days later the gambler returned to the Silver Ring, asking for "one of those sandwiches" he had the other night. Angelo said the sandwich was an extra-large "special," and that he would have to charge fifty cents. "Do it," the gambler insisted, and Angelo's "special" was born.

According to family historian Angelo Spoto, the Silver Ring became so popular for sandwiches that the business could afford to concentrate on food. At one point, the family claims the Silver Ring was the busiest sandwich shop in the country. Customers lined up for a sandwich and looked longingly through the large front window. Inside, a *lonchero* sliced meats for all to see. During his busiest weeks in the 1960s, Cacciatore still sold 8,000–10,000 per week, and 12,000 during Gasparilla. Many considered the Silver Ring to be a local benchmark of consistent quality.[29]

Celebrations such as the Florida State Fair, Latin American Fiesta, and the annual Gasparilla pirate invasion further enshrined the Cuban sandwich, along with deviled crabs and a Sicilian pizza called *scacciata,* as irreplaceable local favorites. The Latin American Fiesta boasted an impressive menu, according to the *Tampa Tribune:* "Spaghetti is a mainstay. Everyone eats pizza. Miles and piles of Cuban sandwiches are consumed."[30]

Gasparilla festivities gave rise to Tampa's biggest picnicking day of the year.

Where else in the country do the natives sit down once a year in chairs several rows deep from one end of the business district to the other and casually break out picnic baskets, oblivious to the hustle and bustle around them. It's a grand sight and it's only fair to give credit where it is due—Gasparilla parade watchers have learned through the years to pack a mean lunch. The Cuban sandwich is the king this day. One reveler had already eaten her Cuban sandwich by 11 a.m., but had brought two.[31]

Heat and pressure took even pedestrian sandwiches to new heights. Restaurants employed small ovens specifically to toast sandwiches, but tailors' irons served as the first sandwich presses in Tampa, providing the heft and direct heat needed to hot-press a Cuban. In the hands of a good *lonchero,* they were also used to sear the exteriors of the roasts and glaze the hams. Pedestrians lingered by the window, drawn by the aroma of caramelized sugar and seared ham. The *Tampa Tribune* observed in 1957:

The reason the Cuban sandwiches of yore tasted so good was due to the ironing of the meat. The ham and pork used in sandwiches of yesteryear had a delicious flavorful coating of caramelized sugar, caused by the branding of the exterior of the roasts with red hot irons. The sandwich maker of those days stood in clean sawdust, making the sandwiches as they were requested. Skilled meat carvers in Latin restaurants today still carve around the meat, shaping it unconsciously in the form of a pear.[32]

The Cuban sandwich expanded in length and girth during the 1950s and 1960s, until every sandwich spot boasted a super-sized "deluxe," "jumbo," or "special" Cuban sandwich. Angelo Cacciatore of the Silver Ring claimed to have invented the "special," but extra-large versions of the sandwich had been prevalent for some time. These robust Cuban sandwiches were marketed as a potential meal rather than a light snack. Rosita's served a "super duper" Cuban sandwich and, according to owner Rosita Sánchez, "it's a full meal in itself." La Brisa Café toasted sandwiches that were fourteen inches long and a full pound in weight. Al's Sandwich and Chicken Center boasted a "jumbo," and restaurateur Ralph Reyes marketed a "large selection of giant sandwiches."[33]

Passersby on Seventh Avenue in Tampa's Ybor City could watch Cuban sandwiches being made in 1966 through a window at the Columbia Restaurant. Courtesy Columbia Restaurant Group.

Frank Klein from the *Tampa Times* theorized on the development of the sandwich, beginning a long line of mythmaking about Tampa's place in that lineage. From the English John Montague [*sic*], the Fourth Earl of Sandwich, it descended to the rest of the world.

The French people substitute small loaves for slices of bread; the Swiss added their famous cheese; the Italians tossed in salami. When the sandwich got to Spain the Spaniards had no buns or small loaves so they used a part of their long loaves sliced lengthwise and called it medianoche, middle of the night or lunch at night. Spaniards had ham and when the Cubans got around to fashioning their own version, they added cheese and several kinds of meat in combination. The addition of the pickle was the American contribution. And Americans want the mustard laid on thick.[34]

According to some locals in Tampa, the old sandwiches in their memory were slathered with butter on the inside, later replaced by mustard.

Tampa Times writer Bob Denley provided his philosophical view of the sandwich.

There are few persons for whom the Cuban sandwich is forbidden: They are the non-hungry, the picky, and those who put form above substance. A Cuban sandwich can be purchased in a size to fit your appetite of the moment. A Cuban sandwich is designed for people who enjoy food, and life itself, to the fullest, without pretense. A Cuban sandwich is to eat. There is only one way to eat it, and that is with gusto.[35]

One of the best accounts of how to make a "real" Cuban sandwich was furnished by the *Tampa Tribune* in 1957. A long-time Ybor City resident and restaurant worker, Manuel Torres, volunteered to make Cuban sandwiches the "old fashioned way" for the newspaper.

Torres soaked a select pork roast overnight in a *mojo* marinade of sour orange, salt, fresh garlic, oregano, and vinegar. He then parboiled the pork with onions, celery, and garlic and then roasted it. A whole smoked ham was then parboiled in the same mixture. Torres trimmed excess fat from the ham and coated it in sugar. He then melted the sugar onto the ham with a hot iron. The resulting caramelized sugar gave the ham a distinctive taste. The salivating reporter noted, "Such an enticing scent rolled up in waves from the meat as the sugar caramelized and hardened into a thin, amber crust! Curious bystanders strolled in from the streets, attracted by the scent."

Torres then carved the meat into thin slices: pork, ham, and peppered Genoa salami. Imported Swiss cheese, sour dill pickles, mustard, and Cuban bread rounded out the sandwich. Each three-foot length of Cuban bread made five sandwiches. The ingredients were layered onto the bread in a specific order: first the ham, then pork, salami, cheese, pickle, and mustard spread only on the top slice of the sandwich. Why? "It is always done that way," Torres said. "That day," the reporter mused, "we ate sandwiches that will never be forgotten."[36]

Tampa loved Cuban sandwiches so much that the rising burger chains had to acknowledge that the hamburger and Cuban sandwich would have to peacefully coexist. Typically a favorite of young people, Cuban sandwiches were a mainstay in Tampa's school cafeterias by the 1950s. Students bought over a thousand a week at Jefferson High School alone in 1962, the only public high school where they were offered all week long at the time. Lunchroom manager Miriam Balderson said, "If we run out of Cuban sandwiches the students jump all over me. You would think that we are completely out of food." Beginning in 1960, students and staff at the newly founded University of South Florida (USF) on the north edge of town dined at a single eatery run by Morrison's Cafeteria. About 1,300 visited the University Center's cafeteria daily, many clamoring for Cuban sandwiches and Spanish bean soup. Dorm-dwellers were especially irritated when USF's administration prohibited Mae's Sub Shop from delivering Cuban sandwiches to campus, probably for competing with the official food service provider, who served more mashed potatoes and meatloaf than anything remotely Cuban.[37]

Carlos Gazitua, Sergio's Restaurant (Miami)

Back in the day, Carlos Gazitua remembered the big show put on by the *lonchero* at his family's restaurant, Sergio's, in Miami. The *lonchero* (or *montador*) would prepare ingredients for the Cuban sandwich—hand slicing the meats, setting out the cheese and other ingredients—then assembled the sandwiches, stacking them in piles at the long counter.

Sergio's traditional recipe uses pork from the leg—not the "wetter" shoulder meat, which Carlos explains they believe should be used for *lechón*. The Cuban sandwich, the family insists, is a deli sandwich; as such, it needs clean slices of meat, which can be had from the leg, but not the shoulder, which shreds like pulled pork. Two generous slices of flavorful leg pork are used in the Cuban sandwich at Sergio's.

Next comes three slices of bolo ham, followed by two Swiss cheese slices. Three to four pickle chips are added, and a smear—not too much!—of mustard on one side of the freshly baked Cuban bread. "My mom," Carlos explains,

For the owner of Sergio's Restaurant, Carlos Gazitua, recipes are built on generations of wisdom. The influence of his *abuela* (grandmother), María Elsa Rodríguez, still inspires his recipes. Courtesy Sergio's Restaurant.

"taught us about the 'surprise element,' that is, you don't necessarily want pickles in every bite—so that when you bite into the sandwich, when you get the pickle, you're happy you got it."

The Cuban bread must be buttered lightly on the outside and pressed on the *plancha* (not a panini grill, which has grooves). The cheese should melt, but the sandwich shouldn't be too hot when served, Carlos insists.

Over the years Sergio's has become an icon in the Miami community, hosting dignitaries alongside everyday folk who have been eating there for years. Carlos's mother, Blanca Cabrera, immigrated to Miami from Santa Clara, Cuba, when Fidel Castro's revolution took control of the island. After finding a little sandwich shop for sale in the outskirts of Miami, called Sergio's, the family purchased it, fixed it up, and kept the name, figuring it was easy to pronounce in both English and Spanish. Eventually Blanca became the first Hispanic woman on the National Restaurant Association Board. Today, her son Carlos follows in his mother's footsteps, serving on the Executive Board of the Florida Restaurant and Lodging Association.

The restaurant has received numerous accolades. Miami-Dade County Mayor Carlos A. Gimenez proclaimed the first day of October "Croqueta Day" in honor of Sergio's serving 20 million of the crispy, creamy Cuban treats. On July 22, 2020, Senator Marco Rubio announced on the Senate floor that Sergio's would be the Senate Small Business of the Week. And during the summer of 2020 when the COVID-19 pandemic was at its peak, the US Surgeon General, Jerome Adams, came to Sergio's to discuss the importance of mitigation efforts, applauding Carlos's measures in keeping restaurant workers and customers safe as he spearheaded the distribution of nearly one million masks to restaurant workers throughout the state.

Today, Sergio's has expanded to thirteen locations and has begun selling and shipping their menu items nationwide. The increasing number of orders and their destinations reveal that Sergio's reach is increasing as each week passes by. Carlos says, "Just this past week we've shipped to twenty states! I get more excited noting the great variation in the states we're shipping to, not just the number of orders. It's great when an order comes in from Tampa or New York, but it's a real thrill when we send a shipment to Idaho!"

Gilbert Arriaza Sr. and Gilbert Arriaza Jr., Gilbert's Bakery (Miami)

The way Gilberto Arriaza Sr. remembers it, the Cuban sandwich—as it is prepared and known today—simply did not exist in Cuba. "The *sanguiche* was a fine thing, a luxury, expensive. It was something that people with economic means often ate after going to the movies late at night. The man would order it with a dark Guinness's Dog's Head stout beer and the woman with a fruit juice or *batido* (a fruit shake typically made with water or milk). That's how the custom became famous."

Today, the Gilbert's family bakery continues the tradition, turning out one of Miami's finest incarnations of the Cuban sandwich. It is a family affair headed these days by Gilberto Arriaza Jr. Father and son explain the components: bread

For Aida V. Arriaza and Gilberto Arriaza Sr., and the Gilbert's Bakery family in Miami, tradition is the backbone of the business. Gilbert Sr. said, "When my children remember something I've taught them—our language, maintaining the idiosyncrasies of our culture—I feel immense pride." Courtesy Gilbert's Bakery.

made with pure lard that, when toasted, becomes crunchy on the outside but retains a soft crumb on the inside; slow-roasted pork spiced with cumin, salt, garlic, and sour orange; sweet bolo ham from local institution Morrison Meat Packers; creamy Swiss cheese; pure butter on one face of the sandwich and a light smear of mustard on the other face; and a few pickle chips, not too astringent.

Although custom and tradition are the backbone of all that Gilbert's does, the family also experiments from time to time. Every Wednesday the twenty-one-person clan gathers at the parents' home to eat, catch up, and talk about new ideas for the family business. That's how the idea of a miniature *sanguiche* Cubano came to be: a tiny version of their original but made with mini Cuban bread about the size of a breadstick. A throwback *emparedado* sandwich with Gouda is in the works. And they are increasing their social media presence, aware that new generations are digital natives who frequent Instagram and Pinterest.

But for all the modernization and experimentation with new ideas, some things stay the same. "I'm very proud," Gilberto Sr. says, "that all the generations in our family speak Spanish. When my children remember something I've taught them—our language, maintaining our culture, the idiosyncrasies of our culture—I feel immense pride."

Ignacio Alfonso Jr., El Artesano Restaurant (Union City, New Jersey)

"¡Finlandia o nada!" insists Ignacio Alfonso Jr., co-owner of El Artesano Restaurant in Union City, New Jersey. The beloved Swiss cheese—a mainstay in many Cubans' kitchens—has the perfect taste and the perfect degree of meltability for the iconic sandwich, Ignacio argues. The restaurateur learned the sandwich-making ropes at the feet of his father, Ignacio Sr., when the elder established the family restaurant in 1974. His father explained that although the name-brand cheese might be a bit more expensive, the finished product would be that much better.

Originally from Unión de Reyes, in Matanzas, Cuba, Ignacio Sr. and his brother Rafael were from a large family of fourteen siblings. They had learned a bit about business by working in a bodega in the "big city," La Habana. There the brothers did a bit of everything—stocking, making deliveries, butchering poultry—and slept in the bodega's warehouse at night to save their money.

Soon Ignacio Sr. saved enough to establish a bar and restaurant in his hometown. His small but growing family moved upstairs above the business. A few years after Fidel Castro's revolution, government officials knocked on their door demanding the keys to the business and gave them an order to relocate. They were grateful when their application to leave the island was approved about two years later. After spending a couple of years in Madrid, Spain, the family finally made it to the United States, finding work in brother Evelio's sandwich shop in Union City.

After a couple of years in the United States, Ignacio Sr., along with his brother, Rafael, established a small eatery, leaving only $100 in their bank account. Realizing they could not afford the cook's salary, they had no choice but to learn how to cook. The rest is family lore.

For Ignacio Jesús Alfonso at El Artesano in Union City, New Jersey, the quality of ingredients was crucial for the creation of a worthy sandwich. Here he appeared with his wife Dulce and the restaurant's Noche Buena (Christmas Eve) pig roasts in the 1970s. Courtesy El Artesano.

Today the restaurant does a brisk business selling traditional Cuban dishes such as *ropa vieja, croquetas,* and yuca. After Ignacio Sr. passed away in 2013, his sons Ignacio and Felix took over El Artesano, modernizing it with computers and incorporating ideas they had from their travels.

The Cuban sandwich at El Artesano has not varied—house-roasted *pernil, jamón dulce* (sweetened with their own glazing syrup), Finlandia Swiss cheese, kosher dill pickle slices, and mustard. The bread, without question, must come from Cuba Bakery—an institution in Union City since 1972. A light brushing of butter on the outside, then pressed in a *plancha*. The finished sandwich, Ignacio Jr. contends, is the same no matter who makes it: "It doesn't matter if the cook is Cuban, Chinese, or Indian; the recipe will never vary."

These days everyone, it seems, has a version of the Cuban sandwich on the menu. Although Ignacio Jr. says none of the ersatz sandwiches are ever truly authentic, he sees it as an opportunity to educate. "It's not at all authentic, they adulterate the sandwich. But I'll take it because when an American comes to the restaurant, it's my opportunity to educate them."

4

Magic Cities

Sloppy in Havana

The United States and Cuba have had a long and troubled love affair. Over time, the occupying *Yanqui* soldiers of old were replaced with a steady stream of tourists. During Prohibition in the United States (1920–1933), thirsty Americans heeded Bacardí's call to find a drink on the island. Those who needed a break from the American Dream could pursue its darker counterpart in Cuba: the American fantasy of the age, which was decidedly masculine and driven by hedonistic impulses. Dry laws in the United States reinforced the *Yanqui's* tendency to see Cuba as a place to indulge. For better or worse, tourists from the United States viewed Havana as a neocolonial playground brimming with a heady brew of free-flowing money, intoxicants, entertainment, and sensuality.

Cuba was the most popular tourist destination in the Caribbean beginning in 1915, a title it would not relinquish until 1930. With its beaches, palms, and cosmopolitan atmosphere, Havana whetted the American appetite for tropical escapades. Many of the hotels and businesses catered to *Yanqui* tastes, from the architecture of new buildings to the food and drink they sold inside. "Americans seek the night life, the false, unreal Havana, and find it," a *New York Herald* journalist acknowledged. Thirsty *Americanos* danced, staggered, and swayed along a sometimes lurid "cocktail trail" of favorite *Yanqui* haunts: the Cuban-American Jockey Club for horse races, cabarets such as the McAlpine for entertainment, the rooftop bar of the Plaza Hotel for vistas, the nameless pornographic movie theater for a glimpse at the forbidden, and so on, all awash with alcohol.[1]

No Cuban institution catered to *Yanquis* more successfully during Prohibition than Sloppy Joe's, an unpretentious bodega-turned-barroom. In 1918, bartender José "Sloppy Joe" Abeal bought a small Havana bodega in an area popular for shopping.[2] Tourists "slumming" around Havana often visited his store for some "local color," and Abeal quickly identified the free-spending *Yanquis* as his best source of revenue.[3] Rather than an admission of dirtiness, people took the name as an invitation to get sloppy themselves, and Abeal capitalized on the traffic by building an open-air bar that faced the street and could be closed at night with a corrugated metal partition.[4]

The jovial atmosphere and extra security helped to make Sloppy Joe's the preferred spot, some said the *only* place, where American women would drink in Havana. "In some way 'Sloppy Joe' has won the tourist trade," an incredulous journalist gasped, "and even dignified grandmothers from Dubuque may be seen on high chairs in Joe's open-faced saloon eating free lunch and sipping 'Presidente' cocktails." Cavorting *Yanqui* women had become a common sight in Havana, where they seemed to "glory in" the Prohibition-era barrooms.[5] A woman who had recently returned from Havana wrote of her trip, "You live like a king here, sleeping when it's hot, imbibing when it's not, and making whoopee in between."[6] In the winter of 1927–28, the Cuba Chamber of Commerce estimated daily arrivals of tourists to be fifteen thousand per day, with most of them arriving in Havana.[7]

In addition to having cheap drinks at the bar, Abeal offered small sandwiches to his guests. It would be easy to assume that picadillo, a seasoned ground beef preparation that often includes olives, raisins, and/or capers, filled those early sandwiches, with its similarity to the version in the United States. Some have claimed that it was *ropa vieja*—or shredded beef—served on a bun. In any case, those saucy beef sandwiches gave succor to many drinkers in need of sustenance who might have otherwise been forced to give up their coveted place at the bar.

Legendary writer and drinker Ernest Hemingway visited frequently, long before he lived in Cuba, sometimes with his bartender friend, Joe Russell, from Key West. When the US Congress repealed Prohibition in 1933, Russell's joint was called the Silver Slipper. Some say that Hemingway had a hand in suggesting the Sloppy Joe's name, but Russell probably stole it on his own initiative. A new legend was born, with a Sloppy Joe's on either side of the Florida Straits. Inspired by the sandwich served by his counterpart down south, Russell created his own variation, a saucy loose-meat hamburger sandwich, dubbing it the Sloppy Joe.[8] Several places in the US Midwest cooked up loose-meat hamburgers at about the same time, later calling them Sloppy Joes, but it all began in Havana.[9]

The Socialite's Sandwich

In 1933, a column in Cuban magazine *Bohemia* suggested sweet sandwiches as an obvious kid pleaser. "Sandwiches are a new invasion in the kitchen of young people and what pleases more than a triangle of toasted bread, cream cheese and compote?"[10] The Elena Ruz has never been quite as famous as its sister sandwiches, but it is still a firm favorite in Miami, and no list of Cuban-style sandwiches is complete without it. In Cuba, the combination of sweet strawberry preserves and cream cheese is akin to peanut butter and jelly for kids in the United States. The addition of sliced turkey in the Elena Ruz gives the creamy-sweet sandwich a savory dimension.[11]

In 1993, *Herald* journalist George Childs dined with Ms. Ruz at Versailles in Miami. There, she told the story of her sandwich's creation in detail. In the late 1920s, Ruz and other students of El Sagrado Corazón school met regularly at a friend's home (the Parraga family's home).

Ruz gathered her friends for high tea on the porches of their families' big houses in the toney El Vedado neighborhood. After going to the cinema, the group usually ended their outing across the street at a café run by a Spaniard named Álvarez. The café became El Carmelo, a fashionable destination. One day in 1927 or 1928 when she was about 18 years old, jaded by Carmelo's lavish menu, Ruz pined for a variation on the flavors of her childhood.

"I asked him to take a medianoche roll, to toast it, then spread strawberry preserves on one side, cream cheese on the other, and in the middle, some of his marvelous roast breast of turkey. I remember going there many an afternoon and describing my concoction to the waiter, to the point that when they saw me coming, they knew what I would order."

The waiters must have been greatly amused and more than a little irritated at the young lady who demanded her childish sandwich in great detail. Rather than simply list the ingredients, her order came with very specific instructions and injunctions.

"Slightly toast the roll before you make up the sandwich, not afterward with all the ingredients in it, already made up. Make sure that you whip or cream the cream cheese, so that it is more spreadable. Spread it on one side of the roll; spread the strawberry preserves on the other side of the roll so that the bread will absorb the taste of the strawberries. Do not place the preserves directly on the cream cheese because it tends to slide off. Make sure you put it on the bread directly. Place turkey in the middle. Don't place too many slices of turkey—it won't be manageable."[12]

After visiting regularly for a year, the students asked if their sandwich could be added to the menu and suggested it be named after its precocious inventor. A friend joked that the sandwich would make Ruz famous one day. Soon after, Ruz went to El Carmelo with her fiancé while her mother chaperoned. They were dumbstruck when they saw the neon sign for the first time that read, "Sándwich Elena Ruz, 25 cents."

"Much to our dismay, there was my name in lights. My mother was somewhat cross. I was so embarrassed at first. I was the talk of the town, everyone was congratulating me and eating my sandwich. Goodness, it was instant fame. I loved it, but my mother was horrified."[13]

El Carmelo was determined to cash in on the sandwich that was now trendy among Havana's young socialites, the kind that did not lack money. The premium on fashion was high when a Cuban sandwich cost ten cents and a medianoche cost only five. "But even so, Elena's mother was outraged, because according to her, it gave the impression that they were selling her daughter for 25 cents."

Ruz's sandwich's legacy was made secure when it appeared in Nitza Villapol's *Cocina al Minuto,* Cuba's national cookbook. Ruz married sugar mill owner Eduardo Ulacia and left for Florida in 1960, where her sandwich had already become part of the landscape of exile. The lady of leisure learned how to cook after emigrating. "I couldn't fry an egg when we arrived in Miami in 1960. In Cuba I'd tell the [domestic] cook to marinate a steak when I didn't even know what a marinade was." While living in Spain during the 1970s, she found her sandwich there as well. She moved to Costa Rica, where she died in 2011.[14]

Memories, however strong, are not always accurate. Armando Villar, formerly a manager at El Carmelo, claims that the restaurant asked Ruz's permission to use her name, while she claims the opposite. The *lonchero* of the Ayestarán Restaurant in Miami claimed the sandwich originated there in the 1960s, a false claim that was easily dismissed. In the 1990s, the *Herald* squashed a rumor that the sandwich had been named after Castro's mother, Lina Ruz. "My sandwich has nothing to do with Fidel Castro," Ruz told the press. "I loathe that man!"[15]

While many eateries proudly offered the Elena Ruz sandwich, its inventor could no longer bring herself to order one. She had been known for dressing down Miami waiters and maître d's for inferior specimens. "They make it terrible nowadays," she groused.[16]

As the journalist's meal with Ruz concluded, a telling incident occurred. After finishing her namesake sandwich, for dessert, Ruz wanted to order off the menu again, just as she did so long before at El Carmelo. Despite the extensive Cuban menu and impressive bakery at Versailles, she called for Italian desserts: *panet-*

tone (a fruit and nut cake) and *tortoni* (an ice cream dessert) mixed in a bowl with chocolate syrup. Ruz was not pleased when Versailles informed her that they did not carry either of the Italian delicacies. The lady with a sandwich named after her was never quite satisfied.[17]

Yanqui Paradise

Even after the United States repealed its prohibition laws in 1933–34, Havana's bars and nightclubs remained a central attraction for tourists from *El Norte*. In 1939, Ernest Hemingway famously settled in Havana for a time to write, fish, and haunt his favorite bars. The Floridita Bar near the old Hemingway home became iconic for its daiquiris. Ernest's wife Mary remembered, "If we stayed late we sometimes dined at the bar on Cuban sandwiches, footlong, crusty delights of Cuban bread sliced horizontally and packed with chicken, ham, pork, pickles, cheese and sausage."[18]

Many Americans heard references to Cuba's delights on the sports page, as the Brooklyn Dodgers spent several seasons of spring training there in the 1940s. Management often fed its players *mixtos*, "a truly monumental piece of work. The Cuban sandwich is a meal in itself, so much so that no Dodger as yet tackled a second helping."[19]

For journalist Bill Cunningham, the sandwich made his list of favorite things in Cuba.

> I love the dreamy sway of the palms, the mockingbird, as that song says, throwing his heart at the sky, the sun, the sand, the nightclub kaleidoscope of satin and sin, the golfer runs packed, the fishing that was always just dandy yesterday or last week, or ought to be better tomorrow. I love the steaks imported from Chicago or Boston, the vegetables from North Carolina, the native strawberries and canned orange juice, the Cuban sandwiches and the condensed milk in the coffee.[20]

For some unadventurous visitors, such as umpire Fred Whittaker, "about the only thing I could stomach was a thing they called a Cuban sandwich which was made out of a couple slices of cheese and ham between two pieces of hard bread; and that fruit cocktail they had was okay at times, but the rest of it, ugghhh." Along with sugar and scenery, the sandwich became a Cuban commodity that was both familiar and exotic enough to market to the bashful palates of some *Yanqui* tourists.[21]

In the 1930s and 1940s, nightlife in Havana grew more opulent to keep pace with the insatiable American fantasy. The glamorous temples to excess competed for the wealthiest patrons with floorshows, burlesque dancing, and big bands galore. Aside from the well-worn Prohibition-era favorites, rising stars included La Zaragozana, El Templete, El Club Vasco, the Zombie Club, and the Riviera Salon Rojo. Havana's most palatial nightclubs and casinos opened after the Great Depression, including the Tropicana, the Montmartre, and Sans Souci (Without a Care).

Exploring Havana's more upscale venues, the *Orlando Evening Star* observed, "We forgot to mention the Flamingo's food. We sneaked to have a Cuban sandwich (they get better and better with every order) and consumed it during the floor show." The journalist recommended eating the sandwich during performances by entertainers, when the lights were darkened and no one could see one's "awkward gustatory jaw movements."[22]

The incomparable Tropicana opened in 1939 and soon became the hottest place in town for wealthy Cubans and foreigners alike. The club sat three thousand guests at a time for its vaunted burlesque floor shows.[23] Places such as the Tropicana symbolized the decadence of Havana, with its music, food and drink, floor shows and black-faced comedy. It took heavy spending to secure a seat at a table, and many Cuban elites tended to identify themselves with the rich *Americanos*.[24]

The *Detroit Free Press* gushed about the Tropicana in 1954:

There is only one sure way to see Havana and that is to go first to the Tropicana. Tropicana is a nightclub, large, lavish and dreamy. The average tourist drifting in with the crowd is surprised to discover a nightclub of such proportions in the heart of quaint Havana. It is equally surprising you find royal palms hovering over your table.

They make the best food this side of grandma's kitchen, whether it be a Cuban sandwich (slices of beef, pork, ham, cheese and pickles between two enormous pieces of Cuban bread) or stuffed swordfish. The visiting Yankee soon learns to distinguish between the strong, black Cuban coffee and "Americano," which is not so strong.[25]

The musical floorshow became one of Havana's most elaborate art forms, an often lurid display for the satisfaction of foreigners. At the Sans Souci, dark-skinned drummers backed a bevy of dancers to conjure a "voodoo ritual." The Tropicana elevated the floor show further, with the finest showgirls and musicians in Cuba. Tucked away in a faux jungle just outside Havana, the Tropicana's "cabaret showcased a kind of sequin-and-feather musical theater that would be copied in Paris, New York and Las Vegas," according to author T. J. English. Other venues off of the main drag featured live sex shows.[26]

Tourism surged again in the 1950s. In Cuba, "no matter where you go you'll bump into an American tourist," the *Miami Herald* observed. "In the heart of the city the air is filled with the monotonous chants of the lottery ticket vendors, the piercing cries and identifying bells of the peanut, ice cream, flower, and vegetable peddlers." Prices had evidently shot up in the overheated tourist economy of Havana, when a journalist wondered, "Why must they charge $1.50 for a Cuban sandwich in Cuba?[27]

One had to exercise some caution when buying sandwiches in public places. Cuban-born writer Enrique Fernández remembered,

> On holidays and carnivals, whenever crowds of people gather, but also at the public parks any day, vendors wander around with baskets full of sandwiches for sale. The bread is in the egg-colored roll and the filling is ham and cheese which has been strategically placed to give the impression of a sandwich so overstuffed the insides are spilling out. It's a trick, my parents tell me. Once you get the sandwich you learn there's practically nothing inside.[28]

Avoiding the convenient vendors roaming the parks, Fernandez's family was very particular about their sandwiches.

> *Sandwiches mixtos* were available at most Havana coffee shops, but true to our vernacular gourmandise, my family had its choice spots. These were mostly Spanish emporia in Old Havana that would have a good selection of wines from the old country. I recalled going to the Spanish taverns at night with my parent, my sister too young to go out at night, often after having watched a movie or two. I just love these sandwiches as I loved all the treats we drove short or long distances to sample.[29]

It seemed that everyone in Cuba was particular about their sandwich vendors, whose creations were suited toward the relative wealth and lifestyles of the customer. José Moreno, a bank employee in the 1950s, recalls the way people sorted themselves between the appropriate cafés. "As one moved upwards in the social ladder of urban distinction, the choice of available food grew in thinness and elegance—by Cuban standards, that is—and sandwiches and *bocaditos* and *pasteles* would metamorphose from one neighborhood to the next."[30]

Although the life of the Cuban Republic (1902–59) was often turbulent, its population rose sharply over the years, from 1.7 million in 1899 to about 7 million in 1959. The rise of a distinct Cuban culture beyond sugar, tobacco, and their derivatives was even more impressive. Cuba's enduring role as a terminus of the Western hemisphere meant it could both absorb foreign influences while disseminating ideas of its own, and Cubans had plenty to say. The world's stage would have to make room for Cuban athletes, thinkers, artists, musicians, and restaurateurs.

The Magic City

The seeds of Miami's Cuban community had been planted in the 1920s, and by the late 1930s, at least six thousand Cubans lived there, with another five thousand around the state. The Latino Méndez restaurant and La Concha both opened in the 1930s.[31]

Miami styled itself as a terminus for travel to South America and the Caribbean. As tourism increased steeply after World War II, the city acquired a reputation for international dining. Restaurante Habana opened in 1946 to serve what was then being called the *colonia latina,* or Latin Colony, a sort of annex to Havana across the straits. "All over Miami I keep seeing a marked Cuban influence," a journalist wrote at the time. The Hispanic culinary scene was dominated by Spanish styles: La Esquina de Tejas, La Covadonga, Vizcaya, and Bilbao, a Basque eatery. Miami's nightclubs could seat twenty thousand revelers with dance floor space to match, a capacity that grew over the following decade. The local music scene became part of a larger South American touring circuit that ran north through Havana. Miami's burgeoning entertainment scene reflected the post-war explosion of Latin American music and dance styles, including the rumba, mambo, and chachachá, all of which were pioneered by Cubans.[32]

Miami became Florida's biggest city in 1950, and in a sure sign that an enclave had settled there, immigrants founded a new chapter of El Círculo Cubano. The social club and mutual aid society was an important beacon of Cuban culture in previous enclaves, such as Key West and Tampa. About 11,600 Cubans lived in Florida in 1950 and another 50,000 visited from the island annually. In 1948, even a young Fidel Castro honeymooned in Miami.[33]

"The foods introduced by the Cubans largely influenced the pluralistic atmosphere," the *Miami Herald* observed. No dish made a bigger impact than the Cuban sandwich. Many journalists would assume over the years that the sandwich did not arrive in Miami until the 1950s or '60s, but it had been in the area since the 1920s, if not earlier. Good Cuban bread could be hard to come by in old Mi-

HELENE POLKA

JUNGLE CLUB

Opposite Jai-Alai—N. W. 36th St. & 37th Ave.

NOW OPEN

MEET HAPPY FROM CHICAGO

DINE & DANCE
UNDER THE PALMS
•
CHICKEN A LA
JUNGLE STYLE
•
CHOP SUEY
•
CUBAN SANDWICHES
•
Fine Wines & Liquors

For Reservations
Phone 8-9147

HELEN POLKA

The Latin jazz craze after World War II packed Miami's nightclubs, which emulated the glamour of those in Havana. Still, a tourist's taste for foreign cultures often ended at the dinner table. Like so many fashionably "exotic" dishes at the time, the Cuban sandwich was a safe choice for less adventurous palates at Helen Polka's burlesque club. *Miami News,* 1946.

ami. Some places used French bread or ordered from Cuban bakeries in Tampa. In the days before national food distributors paid much attention to ethnic products, *pan cubano* arrived via Greyhound Bus.[34]

The first ads for Cuban sandwiches in Miami appeared in the 1920s, and local journalists wrote about yard-long loaves of Cuban bread in the 1930s. Over the years Miami's newspapers seemed terribly out of touch with the Cuban culture in their midst. In 1932, a writer suggested a regrettable Cuban sandwich filling of canned tuna mixed with diced boiled egg, olives, pickles, and salad dressing. In 1946, when the *Miami Herald* published an article about sandwiches, it included a recipe for a Cuban sandwich. Starting with French or Cuban bread spread with butter or margarine, the recipe called for "cold cuts or any sliced meat" topped with "tomatoes, onions, scallions, lettuce, mustard, radishes, cucumbers, cheese—they are all good."[35] In any case, the city of Miami was not yet known for Cuban sandwiches. "Dozens of Miami spots list Cuban sandwiches on their menus," the *Miami News* wrote in 1953, "but we haven't discovered one yet that can approach the [real] McCoy at the Miami Restaurant on Havana's Prado."[36]

Cuban sandwiches were certainly part of the landscape in some form long before 1954, when *Detroit Free Press* journalist Arthur Juntunen enthused about Miami's prospects,

> There may be spots on the vacation map where business isn't so good, but you can't sell gloom to Miami Beach. While the rest of the world weeps, they open up the first strings along the fabulous Florida gold coast. This year there's going to be more beef in the Cuban sandwiches and more vermouth in the dry martinis. There's going to be more of everything, especially more people and more money in the cash registers. The glittering beach already has 378 hotels, most of them super swank, and you'd think that would be enough. But there's another new and bigger hotel going up on Collins Avenue—a 14 million dollar affair called Fontainebleau.[37]

The hotel and resort boom continued into the 1950s, matching Havana's across the straits with Miami Beach behemoths such as the Fontainebleau opening in 1954 and Hotel Eden Roc in 1956. It appeared that Miami was becoming truly cosmopolitan, a domestic tourist destination featuring international flavors, with Cuban and Spanish accents already leading the way.

> If you're dining out in Miami, we've got just about everything in cuisine. Veritably, you can go around the world in 80 dinners. From hamburgers to stone crabs, Miami makes a fetish out of food. Is smorgasbord your dish? There's over a hundred varieties at Old Scandia. Are you a steak and potato paranoiac? Our steakhouses are as numerous and varied as any city in the U.S. How about the Italian influence? There are pizza parlors galore; and scores of Italian restaurants where spaghetti is merely a side dish. French, Scandinavian and German too; and lots of Spanish restaurants. *Arroz con pollo* is for amateurs; the gourmets go for *paella Valenciana*. Cuban sandwiches, day or night. Have you tried Polynesian?[38]

Batista's Final Reign

Since 1920, Havana had marketed itself as a playground for the American fantasy in Cuba, which was on its way to being fulfilled in 1958. Cubans lived in the shadow of America's power and wealth, tantalized by its lifestyle but unable to reap its benefits. American food products and companies began to crowd out the Cuban specialties of Havana. *Yanqui* words, including sandwich, became part of Cuban vernacular. The growing middle class, typified by Havana's suburb of El Vedado, leaned toward American fashions and products. Rich Cubans flaunted their wealth, and the island claimed the world's highest per capita ownership of Cadillacs in 1949. But this wealth at the top only served as a thin, shiny veneer that masked deep problems and popular discontent. In the countryside, nine out of ten were malnourished.[39]

President Fulgencio Batista became the embodiment of Cuba's crooked politics. He rose to prominence in the Sergeants' Revolt of 1933, after which he promoted himself colonel and the head of the armed forces. Content to lurk in the background for a time, Batista was the power behind several puppet presidents. Elected president himself in 1940, Batista oversaw the approval of a new constitution, but he was too eager to please his foreign benefactors. In 1941, Batista struck a deal with the United States to sell Cuba's sugar crop (85 percent of its exports) at painfully low prices, making it all the more difficult for his people to prosper.[40]

On March 10, 1952, former president Fulgencio Batista seized power for a second time when it appeared he would lose the upcoming election. Under his previous leadership as president (1940–44), he indulged the *Yanqui* diplomats and tourists while he neglected (and later bullied) the common people. In addition to its natural beauty, beaches, and cosmopolitan Havana, Cuba lured tourists with the casino gambling, prostitutes, and narcotics that Batista secretly condoned.

El Presidente's inspiration to restart his political career was supplied in part by Meyer Lansky, a Jewish-American criminal mastermind from the days of prohibition. Once president, Batista passed Hotel Law 2074, offering tax incentives, government loans, and casino licenses to anyone who built a hotel costing in excess of $1 million or a nightclub costing $200,000. With no gaming commission and attractive tax breaks, the law practically invited organized criminals to invest in Havana, and they did. Soon practically every major mob boss in the United States could have his own resort in Havana, or at least a piece of one. Havana experienced a building boom like never before. While the mob skimmed money from their businesses and cooked the books, Batista was the man at the top, skimming the state of Cuba.[41]

While *El Presidente* wielded impressive power, he also became associated with Cuba's mounting problems. Batista's violent reaction to opposition disillusioned citizens about his leadership and motives. He found that he did not have enough government positions, hotel-casinos, and shady deals to buy off everyone.[42] Batista failed to grasp the depth of the hunger, suffering, and resentment his system had created. He also underestimated the assertiveness of the Cuban people themselves, who began to mobilize against his regime.[43]

The press in the United States was blissfully unaware of how unstable Cuba had become. Less than two weeks after the coup, a Chicago journalist seemed to relish his assignment to prove that Havana was perfectly safe for tourists.

> Havana, Cuba, March 22. This is being written by the side of the beautiful pool of the famous Nacional Hotel. Except for some small talk, the recent coup of General Batista is ancient history. Unless you go near a military installation or the presidential palace, there is no evidence that a revolution took place on March 10th. So safe for tourists is Cuba that I am here with my wife and nine-year-old daughter, Taffy.

After clearing customs, the journalist and his family sipped complimentary frozen daiquiris and checked into the hotel. Their local guide was a man known as Little Joe,

> [who had a] delightful sense of humor and just right accent. We saw old Havana, ancient churches, including the magnificent Our Lady of Mercy. We ate in various little restaurants, the famous Sloppy Joe's (Cuban sandwiches two inches thick with ham, cheese, etc. are 75 cents), and tried Cuban beer and numerous sidewalk cafes where we were serenaded by wandering troubadours.[44]

In 1955, Hilton Hotels Corporation announced its next monument to the American appetite would be built in Cuba. As construction neared completion in January 1958, Batista announced a three-day fiesta to mark the opening of the Havana Hilton, a $24 million state-of-the-art hotel, the largest in Latin America at the time. The Hilton's entertainment complex boasted two underground garages to hold five hundred cars, a full casino, a large supper club, and six restaurants and bars, including a rooftop bar. The final jewel in the Hilton crown was Trader Vic's, a trendy Polynesian-themed restaurant and tiki bar, the first opened outside the United States. The massive project, which was still not complete on opening day, had been funded by the state-run pension plan of Cuba's catering workers. The behemoth would be operated by the massive Hilton chain, which was credited by some for spreading the "American way of life" to foreign lands. When it opened in 1958, the Hilton was the fourth multimillion-dollar hotel to open in the Havana over the previous six months.[45]

As the Havana Hilton prepared for a succession of star-studded opening parties, the palace of hedonism "looked like Las Vegas on New Year's Eve," but the crowds never materialized. Dark portents had shaken would-be attendees, including President Batista himself. Since 1956, Fidel Castro and his rebels, who vowed to overthrow the government from their stronghold in the Sierra Maestra mountains, supplied the bad tidings.

Norman Van Aken,
Chef and Author (Miami)

A gleam sneaks out from the corners of chef Norman Van Aken's eyes when he launches into a time-soaked anecdote. Even on the phone. You can hear his vocal cords tighten with anticipation. His tone rises a half-octave and then the tale begins and you're in the story boat with him. The world is an ocean of stories for him to sail.

There are warm memories of his days running with Emeril Lagasse and Charlie Trotter as they climbed the culinary ladder.

Then there's the time on New Year's Day in 2002 when he and *New York Times* reporter R. W. "Johnny" Apple Jr., set out on a quest assigned by the newspaper of record: Find Miami's best Cuban sandwich.

Armed with a list of suggested spots and a seemingly unlimited expense account no editor would dare question, Apple and his wife Betsey attempted with Van Aken and his beloved wife Janet to take a one-day bite out of all the city had to offer between crisp slices of *pan cubano*.

"That man took his job seriously," Van Aken says.

Best known for introducing the word "fusion" into the modern cooking lexicon, Van Aken is widely regarded as a founding father of New World Cuisine, which celebrates Latin, Caribbean, Asian, American, and African flavors. He is the

Pioneering Miami chef Norman Van Aken says the Cuban sandwich's success is the amalgam of meat, fat, acid, starch, and sweetness. It hits in a "deep in the gut and deep in the heart way." Courtesy of Norman Van Aken.

only Floridian chef inducted into the prestigious James Beard Foundation's list of Who's Who in American Food and Beverage.

Apple was a political reporter in Washington, DC, and served as bureau chief in Saigon during the Vietnam War, along with writing from London, Moscow, and Nairobi during his forty-three years with the *Times*. In a 2003 profile in the *New Yorker*, Calvin Trillin wrote, "He has a round face and a pug nose that give him a rather youthful appearance; a former colleague once said that when Apple flashes his characteristic look of triumph he resembles 'a very big four-year-old.' His form reflects the eating habits of someone who has been called Three Lunches Apple, a nickname he likes."

On New Year's Day in 2002, the Van Akens caught Apple in mid-gustation.

"He was already on the fourth Cuban sandwich he had consumed that morning," Norman says. "There was sweat on his face. Crumbs on his Polo Ralph Lauren shirt and he was excited. Betsy was in the car at this point. She'd had enough of Cuban sandwiches."

He trampled through Nena's, whose owner "would be a Living National Treasure if Florida were Japan." He devoured Palacio de los Jugos, known for its abundant variety of Cuban food and its tropical fruit juice concoctions. He considered Rio Cristal, known for *palomilla* steaks smothered in avalanches of crispy French fries. He walked and dined among the mirrored rooms at Versailles on Calle Ocho (Eighth Street).

In the end, Apple declared a champ: Latin American Cafeteria on Coral Way. "It proves its superiority more than a thousand times every day, with sandwiches that are just a bit plumper, richer, and cheesier than the competition's."

He suggested enjoying a crusty, shiny version fresh-from-the-press paired with a Hatuey beer or a milkshake made from the vanilla-scented *guanábana,* or custard apple. "You'll see right away why the parking lot is full," Apple wrote.

"It was great to see a man of his experience tackle what was the best Cuban sandwich," Van Aken remembers. "Janet and I only were able to do about three of those places and then had to sail off to work."

That morning was a long way from Van Aken's introduction to South Florida. As a middle child sandwiched between two sisters and an older brother, he would visit Miami Beach with his parents on vacation from their home in Diamond Lake, Illinois. His life only a few miles from Wisconsin contrasted vastly with this summer fun in the sand, the warm sunlight, the smell of suntan lotion, the taste of an ice cream bar. After his parents split and high school turned into college, he hitchhiked his way to Key West, after spending time as a carnival worker and field hand, mowing golf courses and glopping hot tar on roofs.

After arriving in Key West in 1971—"The world's largest open-air sanitarium," he calls it—he found work as a line cook at the Pier House. An avid reader thanks to his grandmother, he began reading James Beard's epic *Theory and Practice of Good Cooking* at the suggestion of a coworker who graduated from the Culinary Institute of America. Where cookbook author and television host Julia Child was a Francophile, Beard explored outstanding food in Texas or Kentucky. Florida, too.

Being self-taught, though, gave Van Aken the license to be inquisitive and explore crossovers in flavors or techniques between Caribbean and classic European cooking that might otherwise have been intimidating. That complex harmony reminded him of jazz, which led to him coining the terms "fusion" and "New World Cuisine."

He doesn't remember his first Cuban sandwich he ate once reaching Key West, but it was likely one purchased at one of the neighborhood laundromats. "I do remember it was cheap and it was filling." On a cook's budget, that was important.

Key West may have been the sandwich's first American home, landing as early as the mid-1800s with Cubans who came to work in the more than two dozen cigar factories on the island. When the cigar factories began migrating to Tampa, the Cuban influence remained.

"One thing you notice in Key West pretty quickly is the very similar nature of the Cuban sandwich, the Media Noche and the Cuban Mix," Van Aken said. "Those are interesting siblings." They all follow the basic tenets of "what makes anything successful, deep in the gut and deep in the heart. The amalgam of meat, fat, acid, starch and sweetness." Finally, the contrasting textures of the crispy bread and the soft interior, which is achieved by pressing.

Tampa can claim the sandwich as part of its identity, he says, but Miami has taken it to heart. Van Aken steers clear of "The ferocious conflict over the rightness or wrongness of salami." He explains:

I don't mind salami on it as long as someone presses it correctly. You definitely will get passionate discourse about Cuban sandwiches in Miami, but I don't think you can discuss food with a Cuban and not get a passionate discourse. They would argue all day about how to make a proper cortadito or a colada or anything like that. My theory on Cuban food and why they are so passionate about it resides in this: When you take away a people's country, which is what happened via Fidel, you hold on to the things you can hold on to. They didn't want anyone [expletive] with their traditions. So Cuban food became very static when it reached the United States and stayed that way until the '90s.

Such rigidity hasn't prevented Van Aken from playing with the form to see where the region's flavors and ingredients would take him. In the mid-2000s, when he and son Justin went back to Key West to open up Tavern N' Town at Beachside, they served longtime Conchs (Key West natives) a version of the Cuban sandwich with caramelized *maduro* plantains spread like mayonnaise. It had pork and ham and mustard and Swiss cheese. But no salami.

"We didn't get a lot of complaints. Got a lot of adherents, in fact."

He prefers nontraditional Creole mustard on the sandwich. The tanginess of vinegar, molasses, turmeric, and horseradish among other herbs and spices gives it a distinct tanginess that cuts through the fat of the pork and ham. "But I won't pass up a Cuban with yellow mustard on it. I like yellow mustard on Cubans."

His allegiances to favorite sandwich shops on the island shift over time:

Our allegiances seem to move. For a long time, it was Sandy's Café inside the M&M Laundromat, where a Cuban Mix with ham, pork, salami, Swiss cheese, lettuce, tomatoes, pickles, mustard, and mayo run about nine dollars. Wild roosters peck at crumbs underneath the red outdoor counter where customers eat on aluminum bar stools.

Lately there's been a new one, though. The Cuban Coffee Queen, named in honor of a woman who taught the owner how to make a proper cafe con leche with toast in Cuba. Their pressed Cuban Mix deviates a bit, giving customers a choice of mojo pork, ham, or mojo chicken as well as onions on the traditional ingredients. Their Cuban Queen Mix goes a step farther, throwing on roasted turkey breast and American cheese.

"They do a nice job with the Cuban there," he says.

And then his questions start. You can hear the eyes crinkle again. Norman wants to compare notes with a friend from Tampa. "Do they have the Mix up there? How about a mollete, a breaded, fried Cuban bread stuffed with picadillo? He never saw one in Miami, but he saw it in Key West in the old days.

"I think there's only one left that makes it," he says with a tone that mixes wistfulness into his curiosity. The search goes on.

Melinda Lopez,
Playwright and Performer (Boston, Massachusetts)

"How can you be from a place you've never even been to?" plaintively asks Melinda Lopez, self-described Cuban-American "playwright, performer, and professor." She poses this in the opening of her critically acclaimed play, *Medianoche/Midnight Sandwich*. Having grown up in the northeastern United States, Boston-based Lopez wrote *Medianoche* before she had ever even been to the island. "Conversations at the table, my mother's cooking, family reunions," she explains, "all of these left a huge imprint on me." It is telling that the play's subtitle is *Or, God Smells Like a Roast Pig,* more than a nod to family gatherings in the backyard of her grandparents' Miami home. The play's narrator reminiscences about the aroma of a pig roast—what her abuelita was doing, what the aunts were doing, the sounds, the smells—for her, the smell is God.

On stage, the narrator makes a medianoche sandwich then eats it, all the while explaining her *cubanidad* to those who have no context. "I have a love affair with the medianoche. We'd go every year to Miami in the summer. It was all about the lechón, the dulce de guayaba, batidos de mamey . . . all the food we could not find in the Northeast. I would contemplate my favorite sandwich, the medianoche, and think: Who would think to put all these elements together in a sandwich? The sandwich sounds like a mess, but it is delicious all together."

Many of Lopez's other plays explore her Cuban roots and culture through a perspective of "bicultural schizophrenia," as she puts it. *Sonia Flew* tells the story of a woman who is a *Pedro Pan,* one of more than 14,000 Cuban children sent clandestinely to the United States in the early 1960s. *Alexandros* focuses on a Cuban family in exile, drawing on the experience of a fifteen-year-old girl visiting her grandmother in Miami, an experience that proves to be a shocking, cross-cultural encounter. *Becoming Cuba,* set in 1898 Havana right before the Spanish-American War, asks: "What does it mean to choose your identity as set from your colonial ancestors?" Like many of Lopez's works, the central character is a strong, uncompromising, and fiercely independent woman.

Today, Lopez stays connected to the island through her work with Boston-area charities that give humanitarian aid to Cuba. She is very involved with Friends of Caritas, an international organization providing support to seniors in

In her award-winning play *Medianoche,* in which she wrestles with the idea of being Cuban without having been there, playwright and performer Melinda Lopez confesses, "I have a love affair with the medianoche [sandwich]." Here, the Cuban American artist appears in her play, *Becoming Cuba.* Photo: T. Charles Erickson, courtesy of Huntington Theatre Company.

Cuba, those with food insecurity, and children with disabilities. Through Friends of Caritas she has traveled to Cuba a number of times.

As for her preferred Cuban sandwich, Lopez believes the simpler the better. "I don't like the new fancy treatments of it," she says. "The croque monsieur version, those with chutney, fancy additions to the mustard. . . . I like it wrapped in paper, cut in half on the diagonal. And no salami!"

Michelle Bernstein,
Cafe La Trova (Miami)

For award-winning chef Michelle Bernstein, the Cuban sandwich was a kind of babysitter when she was growing up in Miami. Once a week, her mother would take her shopping at El Eden, a small cafeteria-grocer across the street from her elementary school.

"Mami would put me in the little bar at the counter and the woman behind it would make me a Cuban sandwich," she remembers. "I would have my banana milkshake and Mami would shop. That's how she would get her shopping done, by putting me at the food counter. She would do the shopping and then scoop me up before we went home."

It's the sort of warm, happy memory that inspires the melting pot of family flavors Bernstein brings to her cuisine, which weaves through her Argentine, Russian, Italian, and Jewish roots as well as the spice of growing up in Miami.

"I am a melting pot," she says. "I feel like we're all melting pots. We're all a big, beautiful mix of something."

In her childhood memories of Miami, there were never any differences in Cuban sandwiches between the restaurants they visited. It was always the foil around the plancha. It was always the same pickle, the same bread.

"But what I liked, though, is that whenever they made you a Cuban sandwich, they'd pull a fresh loaf out of the paper and pick out the little piece of palm leaf that used to be in there. They'd pull that out, they'd cut it fresh and they'd fill it with all the goodness. Always the same stuff."

It is a perfect sandwich, she says. It has everything a person would want. It is easy to eat. It is between two slices of bread that doesn't really fall apart. It is warm and gooey. It has everything you need. It has a beautiful flavor and even though you have so many ingredients, you can still taste the mojo and then you can taste the pickle and then, lightly on the edge of your tongue, you can taste the mustard.

"You might change ingredients and get fancy and add a parma or prosciutto instead of a ham, or a pork belly instead of a lechón, but you'll always have that magical combination of flavor and texture that goes beyond comparison to anything," she says.

On fancy nights during her childhood, the family would go to dinner at Islas Canarias, which is still around. It remains her favorite classic Cuban restaurant in Miami. She also grew up ordering at the window at Versailles Restaurant on Calle Ocho in Little Havana.

Where she never had them: At home.

The reasons: First, she's not Cuban, although she admits, "We'd make *choripán* (chorizo sandwiches) at home."

Second: It's a lot of work. Who the heck wants to roast pork themselves, get the sliced ham and cheese and the right kind of bread?

Then there's the griddle. If you don't have the right kind of griddle, you'll never make the best Cuban sandwich.

"It's just too many ingredients to put together at home," Bernstein says. "When you can get it cheaper from a little Cuban shop, why bother?"

The closer you get to Dade County and, specifically Little Havana, the more the sandwich evokes emotions. Bernstein knows this. It's why she called her version "My Untraditional Cuban."

"For me to do a traditional Cuban sandwich, and for me to be the melting pot that I am, it really doesn't make sense," she says. "I'm thinking of taking it off the menu because a lot of Cuban people come to our establishment and expect a great, traditional Cuban, and I don't think I could give it to them in the way they were brought up eating it."

Bernstein's deviation from tradition starts with the mustard, a combination of yellow, Dijon, and mustard seed. She mixes that with mayonnaise—another perceived traditionalist sacrilege—and then adds diced roasted jalapeños for spice, which is sure to turn the heads of traditionalists.

Now, Cubans don't like heat. They also get pissed off when I use a little bit of hot sauce in my arroz con pollo. Again, I'm not saying, or haven't said, that I'm Cuban or cook Cuban. I do know how, and if someone asks me to make a Cuban sandwich that doesn't have the frills of being a chef, I would make it the way I had it growing up. Absolutely. Or if I was making it for someone who had only been here the first time, I would make them a traditional Cuban, and I know very well how to do it. I just take the option of making something I also enjoy eating the most.

I get nervous when Cuban people come in to eat because I know what's going to happen. They're going to be, "That's not how I grew up eating it." But I'm always very open that I'm not pretending to be your mother's cuisine or your grandmother's. I would never take that place. I would never want to, because I would never want someone to take my mother's place either. No one is going to make me empanadas like my mother did.

The Cuban would be nearly unrecognizable to traditionalists in her 2008 cookbook, *Cuisine a Latina: Fresh Tastes and a World of Flavors from Michy's Miami Kitchen* (Rux Martin/Houghton Mifflin Harcourt). She upgraded the mainstay of Swiss cheese to gruyere. She wanted something that melted a little more.

"I was really into 'fast' back then as a chef," she said. "Over time, you start taking the bacon out and the duck fat out and you realize you don't need truffles. Little by little, you start cleaning up your act. You don't have crutches anymore. You don't need the gruyere."

That's not to say the sandwich shouldn't evolve, she says. The fact that the Genoa salami didn't migrate to Miami from Tampa fascinates her. "According to Miami there is no rivalry [over the sandwich]. According to Miami, people from Tampa are crazy. It's not even something people talk about. It's a dead subject. This is how you do a Cuban and that's it. There is no other. It's a very Miami way to be."

Bernstein closely follows new variations of sandwich ingredients and techniques introduced by chefs. She has also watched the sandwich migrate to Miami's suburbs. "Because the Cubans have now done well and moved on [to other professions], maybe they're not the ones who fix the sandwiches anymore."

Recently, she and a colleague went to a shop to buy sandwiches and she noticed a different way of making them. The results were delicious. She could still taste the lime and mojo in the pork. But it was a different brand of pickle. And they applied it differently. The sandwich makers opened the press and put the pickles on at the end—which in her mind was a better idea because they stay fresher.

Bernstein: And these were Venezuelan women doing it. "The Nicaraguan women do it differently. Everyone whose hand is taking the place of a Cuban's hand is changing the Cuban a little bit. To a blind eye, to a person, say, from Milwaukee, it would be the same Cuban sandwich they would either dream of or tasted once on a vacation in South Florida. But I know, because I grew up on this, that things have definitely evolved.

It's so funny how so many great memories are born and bred of Cuban flavors. Instinctively because that's who we are. The whole thing about it, the Cubans have come and gone—they're still here in a very strong Cuban community, but they moved on to more suburban areas—but they've left such an imprint, the Columbians, the Venezuelans, and the Nicaraguans and even the Argentines, we're all making Cuban-style food. Obviously it's had a lasting impact that will always be here.

Cuban DNA is embedded in the genetic code of Miami. We are literally a boat ride away. Not only our food, our style of clothing, our music, our way of speaking Spanish. We are very Cuban. There are Cubanisms in the way we speak. You're going to dance hopefully as well as a Cuban might. And you'll definitely be tempted to smoke a cigar a few times in your life and sit with a glass of good rum. Even if you've never been there and you're from Miami, you probably speak Spanish like a Cuban.

It makes sense living in Miami that you would eat like a Cuban.

"We are heavily influenced by everything Cuban," Bernstein says. "It's not just the Cuban sandwich."

Cuban Sandwich from Cafe La Trova

Yield: 3–4 Sandwiches

Roast Lechón

1 cup cilantro leaves, or 1½ cups cilantro leaves

1 cup parsley leaves

5 garlic cloves, smashed

2 tablespoons ground cumin

1cup lime juice

1 cup orange juice

1 boneless pork shoulder (3 to 4 pounds), cut into 4 pieces

Salt and black pepper

Combine all ingredients except pork shoulder, salt, and pepper in the bowl of a food processor and pulse until combined but not totally smooth. Rub the pork shoulder pieces with the marinade, cover and allow to marinate overnight in the refrigerator.

Heat oven to 275 degrees. Remove the pork from the refrigerator about 1 hour before cooking, to come to room temperature. Place pork on a baking sheet and season heavily with salt and pepper. Cover with aluminum foil and bake until it reaches an internal temperature of 200 degrees, about 2½ to 3 hours, or until a fork inserted into the pork can be rotated 90 degrees with little resistance.

Remove the pork from the oven and allow to cool enough to handle. Shred the meat, discarding any skin or fat. Strain the cooking liquid, skim off and discard any fat and mix a little of the juice with the cooked pork. Season to taste with salt and pepper.

Mustard Sauce

1 cup mayonnaise

¼ cup Dijon mustard

2 tablespoons yellow mustard

1 jalapeño, roasted, peeled and seeded, chopped fine

Mix all ingredients together.

The Sandwich

1 loaf Cuban bread, cut open lengthwise

1 to 1½ cups roast lechón, warmed

8–10 slices Swiss cheese

8–10 slices serrano ham

12–16 slices bread and butter pickles

4 tablespoons mustard sauce

1 tablespoon unsalted butter, softened

Spread about 2 tablespoons of mustard sauce on each side of the bread. Layer the serrano ham on the bottom piece of bread, with each slice slightly overlapping the previous. Top with about 2 cups of the pulled pork. Top with cheese and pickle slices. Close the sandwich.

Cut the sandwich into 3 to 4 portions. Spread about 1 teaspoon of butter over the top of each sandwich and wrap tightly in aluminum foil.

Heat a griddle or large pan over low heat. Place wrapped sandwiches on the pan, press with a heavy skillet, and heat for about 5 to 6 minutes on each side. Carefully remove foil and serve!

5

Exile and Resilience

The Cuban Revolution

Throughout the Cuban republic, university students became one of the few strident political voices calling for reforms. A variety of ideologies vied for power in the 1930s and 1940s, especially Communism and the Cuban tradition of *gangsterismo,* or political factions backed up with deadly force. From their ranks, a young radical law student rose with the daring, rhetoric, and *gangsterismo* swagger to bring down Batista. After a failed attempt to overthrow the president on July 26, 1953, Fidel Castro was released after a brief stint in prison, only to return with a band of armed rebels in December 1956. Despite a desperate beginning, Castro's small force found refuge in the Sierra Maestra mountains, nurtured by sympathetic peasants and largely ignored by Batista until it was too late. Wavering support from the United States doomed the regime. In December 1958, the maligned Batista fled with $300 million (valued at $2.7 billion in 2020) of his people's hard-won currency to live in isolated luxury.

On January 1, 1959, Castro assumed control of Cuba and quickly stifled opposition. The Havana Hilton, which had opened just nine months before, became the revolution's headquarters where he conducted the affairs of state. The exodus of Cuban exiles recommenced on a massive scale.

Many Americans were caught in Cuba during Castro's takeover, and the US Embassy struggled to house and feed them during the crisis. Journalist LeRoy Hayes, who traveled to Cuba routinely before, complained when Cuban authorities started to round up Americans on New Year's Day 1959. First, police sent them to the Hotel Sevilla-Biltmore. The next day they moved them to the Hotel

Nacional. "They didn't provide any food," Hayes wrote, "and when I finally arrived at the Nationale [*sic*] Saturday there were about six hundred sleeping outside on a lawn. It was like living in jail at the Nationale [*sic*] for Americans. The Christmas season is usually gay here, but it was unusually quiet." Hayes managed to find a Cuban sandwich and three bottles of beer in a café.[1]

At the meeting of the Pan American Round Table in El Paso, Texas, members read the letter of Johnny Ouida, a member who wrote from the island. He was commended by the U.S. ambassador for his work as part of the Immigration and Nationalization personnel in helping to evacuate two thousand American tourists from Cuba. "It was a most orderly revolution; television, lights, water and phones were operating around the clock. It was fun watching the *barbudos* (bearded ones) on TV giving their names and hometowns and telling mama, papa and wives they were alive and well. I have had a Cuban sandwich, and I'm all for it. It had enough ham and cheese between a French roll to make ten American sandwiches!"[2]

For journalist Jules Dubois, who ran afoul of Castro for some unflattering press coverage, the Cuban sandwich was a tender mercy. Castro ordered several labor unions, which suddenly answered to the state, not to serve the offending writer. No one at the Hotel Havana Hilton would serve him, despite being a guest there. Dubois called it a "Cold War" waged against him personally. The elevator and telephone operators soon relented in helping him. The food and beverage manager discreetly sent Cuban sandwiches and coffee to his hotel room.[3]

A group of journalists spent a day in March 1959 waiting to see Castro at his personal headquarters, located in a rented suburban villa in the hills. After making them wait for most of the day, Castro's staff served what must have been the most joyless Cuban sandwich reception ever given on the island, with Castro still absent.

Though the men with their beards and the women in uniform, many carrying tommy guns [Thompson Submachine Gun] or pistols, are extremely, even excessively picturesque, it would not be right to speak of a comic opera atmosphere. Everything was too serious for that. We strolled in and out of the pleasant little villa or sat under trees outside. About half past two, food came. It had been ordered in from Havana [and] consisted of trays of Cuban sandwiches, made out of French bread sliced horizontally and containing a slice each of cheese, ham and chicken. Then came more trays of Cokes and the spirits of the partakers rose somewhat.[4]

When Castro finally deigned to appear before the journalists, he passed through like a hurricane, which was typical of his style. Although ostensibly a student of law in 1948, Fidel Castro absorbed the lessons of gangsterism all too well. He did not simply enter a hall or room; he seized and occupied it. His epic, ranting speeches to supporters eviscerated enemies—none more than the United States—but did not always translate into coherent policies, leading the *Tampa Tribune* to editorialize, "Cubans are a warm and demonstrative people, who naturally dramatize situations, but it seems to us that Fidel Castro is overdoing it. The high melodrama down Havana way gets thicker than a Cuban sandwich." Instead of bringing Cuba the salvation he had promised, Castro brought repression, Communism, Soviet aid, and the everlasting ire of the United States.[5]

The United States severed relations with Cuba on January 3, 1961. The broken relationship went from bad to worse in April, when the US military landed an invasion force of several thousand armed Cuban insurgents at Playa Girón on the east bank of the Bay of Pigs hoping to prompt a popular uprising against Castro. The plan, which had been cooked up by the Central Intelligence Agency, assumed that the president would openly back the rebels if they ran into difficulties. The open participation of the US military could have led to war with Cuba and the Soviet Union. Faced with this dangerous escalation and with no contingency plans provided by the CIA, President John F. Kennedy aborted the operation. As a result, Castro's army crushed the would-be invasion, leading to the capture of about 1,200 volunteers, mostly Cuban exiles. This event led many Cuban exiles to distrust the Democratic Party and favor Republicans. The CIA escaped blame for the deeply flawed plan. It would not be the last time Kennedy rebuffed the advice of military advisors to wage war against the Soviets over Cuba. *The Pittsburg Press* noted dryly just after the fiasco, "While Fidel Castro was having a picnic warring on the rebel invasion force [at the Bay of Pigs], a Pentagon commissary menu entreated its military customers to enjoy a Cuban sandwich with coleslaw, 65 cents."[6]

As waves of indignation rippled across the United States against Castro, the Cuban sandwich became something far too enjoyable for such a name. The *Detroit Free Press* reported that the Devon Gables restaurant had "severed relations with Cuba. What used to be the Cuban sandwich on their menu is now dubbed the Caribbean." In Jacksonville, two eateries announced name changes, opting for the Latin American or Americana sandwich. A third sandwich maker disagreed with the name change, as it "wouldn't be fair to the honest people in Cuba." The Old Colony Restaurant in Tampa rechristened their sandwich the Cuban Bomb.

"Anti-Castro feeling got so bad in Tampa's Ybor City," the *Orlando Sentinel* observed, "that some cafe owners who had specialized for years in Cuban sandwiches began advertising Spanish mixed sandwiches." Tom Inglis wrote in the *Tampa Times,* "If this is disloyalty, so be it—but I'm opposed to this Castrophobiac move to change the name of the Cuban sandwich. I don't think it will ever sell."[7] Quik Snak in Largo named its sandwich after the Bay of Pigs.[8]

After fielding complaints for years at the Pentagon's cafeterias about the name of the sandwich, "Patriots started calling it a Castro burger. Yesterday John Horn, the cafeteria manager, capitulated," the *Kansas City Times* wrote in 1962. "The roast beef, Swiss cheese, Lebanese Bologna, Danish ham, kosher pickle and long roll combination appeared on the menu as the U.N. sandwich."[9]

Canadian missionary Reverend B. G. Leonard traveled to Cuba in July 1962 and was deeply shaken by the scene there. Everywhere he saw serious faces and the militarization of society. Leonard returned to Havana's famous eatery, the Miami Restaurant, which was renowned for quality, and got another surprise when he was served a plate of inferior rice with flecks of something that may have been meat. This cost him 2.50, which was no bargain at the time. He then remembered the famous Cuban "Dagwood" sandwich that was served for fifty cents just a few years before.[10]

Just as the United States had shut down the Cuban lottery and banned cockfighting and bullfighting when it administered Cuba, the revolution cleansed the island of its casinos, brothels, and the lottery, which had all been reintroduced with a vengeance. Prostitutes and other employees protested that they were being thrown out of work, so Castro delayed the order until alternative employment could be found for the refugees of vice. The mafia based in the United States lost its overseas empire virtually overnight. A new law stating that only Cubans could own property on the island was far more troubling to legitimate US business interests. Tourism plunged from about 180,000 visitors in 1959 to about 4,200 in 1961.[11]

Government planners announced in 1961 that ten years later, Cuba would have a standard of living that would rival that of Europe and outclass the rest of Latin America. An ambitious government campaign taught the illiterate to read and write in a single year, but the revolution faltered in most other respects. It soon became apparent that socialism was incapable of producing a good Cuban sandwich or much else worth eating. In the spring of 1960, shortages already pinched the Cuban food supply. In 1962, the government began rationing food, clothing, and other goods. Peasants who no longer had to pay rent had little financial motivation to raise more crops, and all the experienced managers had fled.[12] Revulsed by Western-style markets and banks, Castro made Cuba's survival almost entirely dependent on Soviet aid despite efforts to diversify.[13]

The *libreta* (ration coupon book) first appeared in 1962, offering monthly six pounds of rice, five ounces of coffee, five pounds of sugar, half a pound of lard, and a pound of beef per adult. The revolution also adopted a stew called *caldosa* as its signature food served at block parties sponsored by the state. Much like the collective *ajíaco* of the Taino Indians and the *sancocho* that nourished the Mambí soldiers fighting against the Spanish, neighborhoods gathered around huge pots of root and green vegetables, holding fiestas with limited ingredients. The Communist state never embraced the Cuban sandwich, perhaps for being too individual and private, or because the state could not afford to serve them at collective block parties.[14]

In place of financial markets, the revolution relied on a "moral economy" fueled by volunteer labor of the "New Cuban Man" in search of national self-sufficiency. Any chance of finding decent food made by enterprising merchants disappeared with the last of the privately owned corner shops (*tencens,* the Cuban variation of five-and-dime or "ten cent" stores) and restaurants during the state's 1968 "Revolutionary Offensive" campaign. Thereafter, Cubans could only spend from their ration books at *bodegas* run by the government.

Those with the courage to emigrate faced the scorn of their neighbors and authorities. They were only allowed to carry five dollars and thirty pounds of luggage out of the country. All other currency, along with any jewelry or other valuables, would be confiscated by the government or stolen by its minions. Police typically strip-searched, harassed, humiliated, and intimidated every prospective émigré as a matter of sport. By 1969, four hundred thousand Cubans, roughly 18 percent of the population, mostly white and middle to upper class, had fled the revolution. On the island itself, the drain helped supply a siege mentality while reinforcing the sense of equality among those who remained. Still, the exodus was far from over.[15]

Out of the first twenty-one hijackings on US airlines after 1961, twenty were diverted to Cuba by political dissidents looking for a safe haven. It became so common that by 1968, airline pilots flying in the American south tucked away maps of Havana's Martí Airport for such an emergency. The Cuban government even instituted a lunch system to supply wayward pilots with Cuban sandwiches upon arrival. Starved for currency, Cuba billed the US State Department a whopping $35 per sandwich, or $265 in 2020 prices.[16]

In the early 1960s, the Cuban sandwich was already a cultural fixture in Miami. Everyone—even the Highview Drug Store—wanted to get in on the action, especially in the weeks leading up to the Orange Bowl football game. *Miami News*, 1961.

Exodus and Exile

In a little over a decade after Castro's rise to power in 1959, Cuban exiles wove a new social fabric into the heart of Miami. A merchant at the time said, "The Cubans have saved downtown" from neglect, opening fruit stands, groceries and restaurants at a time when urban centers in America were faltering. The omnipresence of Cuban cafés led the *Miami News* to declare that Cuban sandwiches had taken over Biscayne Boulevard. "We're finally getting a balanced group of fine eating places and none too soon."[17]

When the *Miami News* reminded readers of the virtues of Cuban immigrants, cuisine led the argument.

> Cubans bring to us time-honored traditions and a rich culture. After all, Havana was known as the Paris of the Americas. Cuban exiles brought with them a wonderful cuisine which we are free to explore. There are any number of little places offering *fritas* [Cuban style hamburgers], rice and black beans or tasty Cuban sandwiches (which, served hot and crusty, must be among the greatest national dishes).[18] Cuban restaurants are another world.

Again two years later, the *Herald* appealed to readers' appetites to soothe ethnic tension. "Our Cubans improve our cosmopolitanism. Visitors from the north want to eat in Cuban restaurants, go to Cuban nightclubs and snack late on Cuban sandwiches. We're happy to oblige and make our own discoveries at the same time."[19]

The restaurant and nightclub operators with the means to relocate crossed the straits to Miami. The wealthiest Cubans had the most to lose and the most resources to relocate, so it makes sense that Miami's most beloved restaurants and nightclubs, such as the Floridita, were transplanted by the same people who ran their predecessors in Cuba before the revolution. Sorrento's, La Floridita, Raul's and many more arrived directly from Havana.[20]

Gustavo Cachaldora, president of the corporation that owned iconic upscale destinations such as La Zaragozana, El 1830, and Les Violines in Havana, watched as the Castro regime assumed operation of his nightclub empire, frustrating his ambitious plans to open a casino. Instead, with his partners, Cachaldora opened new palaces of leisure in Miami, including Les Violines Supper Club and the Flamenco Supper Club.[21]

When brothers Roberto and Orestes Lleonart came to Miami in 1966, they opened a Latin supermarket. Over the next decade, they worked grueling hours and gradually bought up an entire city block. In 1975, they opened Ayestarán, a restaurant that quickly became known for good food, friendly service and reasonable prices. Sandwiches became a mainstay, and the Ayestarán became known as a favorite of celebrities, including an appearance in the movie "Miami Rhapsody." It closed in 2013 after almost fifty years of service.[22]

One of Miami's earliest documented Cuban sandwich purveyors, Frank Garcés, immigrated to New York City in 1927. When he moved to Miami twenty years later, he opened the Do Drop Inn, a bar that sold hot, pressed Cuban sandwiches. The item sold so well that he put up a sign claiming his restaurant as the "home of the Cuban sandwich." In 1949, he relocated to a bigger bar at Northwest Seventh Avenue and Twenty-Sixth Street, which he converted to a Spanish-American restaurant called Knife and Fork. His sandwiches attracted a largely "American" crowd by the time of his retirement in 1969.[23]

The *Miami Herald* traced its "King of the Cuban sandwich," Francisco "Paco" Aparicio, to a café in the Havana suburb of El Vedado in 1953, where he ran a popular sandwich stand. Residents there loved to stop for a bite, especially while taking their Sunday promenades. Aparicio expanded the sandwich stand, and by 1958, the shop was the stuff of Havana legend. After Castro's revolution, Aparicio fled to Miami, where he practiced his craft at the Casablanca in the 1960s. Aparicio's secrets: "crispy Cuban 'water' bread, baked that same day; boneless processed ham cured in boiling hot sweet water and baked in sugar at 250 degrees; pork roasted slowly with the right amount of seasoning; imported Gruyere Swiss cheese; pickles; butter." He warned others never to use machines to slice the meat but did not state why. In 1975, he sold four thousand sandwiches per week, mostly on Sundays, when $1.55 bought a half-pound Cubano, while twenty cents more got a "special" weighing 12 ounces.[24]

Cubans and their sandwiches had quickly become an essential element of Miami's identity. In 1966, the *New York Times* described the bustling midtown area of Miami around Gesú Catholic Church (First Avenue and North East Second Street):

> This area harbors several short order restaurants at which yard-long Cuban sandwiches are sold. Ham, turkey, pork loin, Swiss cheese, pickles and mustard are layered on a long loaf of crusty white bread (similar to French bread) and then cut into about four sandwiches. Prices start at $0.50. It is a noisy, cluttered, highly commercial district.[25]

The Cuban infusion had revived the flagging fortunes of the dilapidated neighborhood along what would be known as *Calle Ocho* (Eighth Street), a bustling promenade that could almost compete with those of Havana. The Badía Restaurant offered sixteen different types of Cuban sandwiches. An improvised bazaar of street vendors sold pastries, religious idols, antiques, and fresh juice.[26]

Refugees who fled the island often found sandwiches at the end of their ordeals. The Freedom Tower still looms large in the minds of Cuban immigrants, a Lady Liberty in Miami pink. In 1962, President John F. Kennedy approved the renovation of the old *Miami News* building to become the Cuban Assistance Center. Federal authorities processed refugees in the seventeen-story "Freedom Tower." Tens of thousands of new arrivals were given peanut butter or ham and cheese sandwiches as their first meals there. One refugee noted that when she received a ham and American cheese sandwich with a muffin and weak coffee, she said that it "seemed to me the 'delicacy of the gods.'" She could only wonder the joy she would have felt if she was served "*the*" Cuban sandwich instead. The government ended operations in the tower in 1974, but it remains a revered historic landmark and museum today.[27]

By the 1970s, residents in Miami-Dade and beyond recognized that the landscape had permanently changed. Cuban immigrants settled into neighboring communities such as Miami Lakes, Coral Gables, Sweetwater, and Hialeah as well as Broward and Palm Beach counties to the north. Miami had more than two hundred Cuban restaurants, with more street food vendors, bodegas, and

In this ad from 1981, El Carmelo Restaurant in Miami evoked the old classic in the Vedado neighborhood of Havana. The new eatery offered all the classic sandwiches, including the Elena Ruz, which was invented at the original El Carmelo location in Havana. *Miami Herald,* 1981.

nightclubs, many selling Cuban sandwiches in addition to their other wares. Some argued that the "authentic" flavors could not be found in the high-end nightclubs or the expensive restaurants, but the more humble joints of Little Havana. "There is no way of really grasping the flavor of the area unless the visitor is willing to get out of his air-conditioned gas guzzler and rub elbows with the [new] natives," the *Miami Herald* advised. A US-sponsored Cuban Resettlement Program found jobs for over half of the exiles by 1974, most of them going to New York, New Jersey, and California. Whether they later returned to Miami was another matter.[28]

The Sandwich in Exile

As South Florida's exile population grew, its collective clout and purchasing power persuaded the *Miami Herald* to create the Spanish-language *El Miami Herald* in 1977 (rechristened *El Nuevo Herald* in 1987). Often featuring Cuban writers, the Spanish-language *El Herald* is an important source for understanding the exile community in the 1980s and 1990s. In its pages, the journalists and community engaged in an ongoing dialogue, a negotiation for what was acceptably Cuban and what was worthy of remembrance and celebration from the old country. What does this source tell us about the sandwich?

The origin stories are murky, but exiles conceded that Cuba was late in joining the great global sandwich game. "Cuba would not be left behind. The sandwich, in our own way, it was an extraordinary reality! Our sandwich!"[29] "The Cuban sandwich was invented by the Cubans and exported to the United States at the beginning of the exodus. The Cuban Sandwich—in fluted bread, with mortadella, pork leg, pickles, and other delicacies—has conquered the North American palate." In this quote, the author mentioned mortadella, which was no longer commonly used in the exile sandwich.[30]

Intense peer pressure often enforced exile norms without any need for debate or conflict. This extended to the sandwich. "It caught my attention that a single reader reminded me that the sandwich in Cuba was also made with mortadella," George Childs wrote, "but I didn't mention that either, because it hasn't been incorporated here." The mention of mortadella by the journalist might have drawn opposition as a challenge to the exile's streamlined version of the classic.[31]

Childs also questioned the assumption that Cubans brought the sandwich to the United States in 1959. "With the influx of Cubans in Miami, it is hard for me to believe that the first Cuban sandwich was not discovered until 1959." The search was on to identify the first Cuban sandwich purveyor in Miami.[32] Others pointed out that the sandwich, "despite its name, since the 1960s has been practically only eaten in the geography of exile."[33] This proud and wistful passage conveys the bittersweet memories of exiles.

> In our very slang we invented the name *lonchero,* the man who made the sandwich. Remember on those counters the square space, all in glass, under which were the ham, cheese, cucumbers, suckling pig, etc., all the *ingredients* for the sandwich. . . . And engraved, in the same glass, the word *lunch.* With the freedom to say: "lonchero, one to go, and one medianoche to eat here."[34]

This quote emphasized the simple perfection of old Cuba, which crops up repeatedly in exile discourse:

> Of course, what we now call a Cuban sandwich we knew simply as a sandwich. It was a bigger sandwich than normal, reserved for birthday parties and gatherings like that. The *bocadillos* were made with a variety of spreads. The Cuban sandwich that I remember was much smaller than the one you eat in Miami. They were more compact, crisp, tasty. Simply much better. The basic ingredients were natural, without chemical additives or flavor enhancers. Then there was the bread. Completely different.[35]

Along with an ideal sandwich, *El Herald*'s readers and writers also identified the ideal purveyor, Havana's Bar O.K.:

> There was never another, among Cuban sandwiches, equal to that of Bar O.K. in Republican Cuba. The sandwich had no rivals and was sold, by the thousands, daily, at that modest corner of Zanja and Belascoain. An "OK sandwich was an outstanding sandwich." The creation passed from father to son. With bread from La Gerona and from a French bakery. They placed the breads, to keep them warm, on the ovens where the pork roasts and hams were roasted, sweet hams that they prepared, slicing the quantities as they were making the sandwich.
>
> Everything was so perfect that each sandwich was a true work of art. They prepared the pork legs (*lechón*), they stabbed the meat to introduce the garlic sauce, and the roast was over low heat. The sandwich came out with the hot lechón, also the ham. And in those days the biggest cost only 75 cents!
>
> It was interesting to see, late at night, how luxurious cars of important people stopped by the Bar O.K. to buy the sandwich. There, in addition, "the best flans" in the city were savored. Many drank a beer or downed a Cuba Libre, patiently waiting for their turn: "Give me four to go."[36]

The storied Bar O.K. attracted an influential clientele. When Cuban Minister of Education José Manuel Alemán traveled to Miami in the 1940s, he urgently ordered sandwiches to be delivered from the bar by airplane.[37]

Late at night, a different kind of desperation ruled in Havana, when men feverishly sought sandwiches for wives and lovers. A favorite Cuban folk tale was "the persuasive power of the sandwich." For example, the tendency for husbands out too late at night to buy domestic peace by arriving home with a sandwich. Men in the worst kind of trouble resorted to getting the best remedy at the Bar O.K. Expectant mothers were known to compel their men to leave the house late at night for such a sandwich run "with plenty of pickles." Superstition foretold that anyone who denied a pregnant woman her food of choice would suffer a painful sty in their eyes, making the search for an OK Bar sandwich all the more stressful for the mates of expectant women.[38]

For all of its efforts to cover Cuban content, the *Nuevo Herald* often overlooked those who came before the late 1950s. For example, a journalist claimed the sandwich was unknown in Orlando, Florida, until José Luis Crespi opened Joe's Sandwich Shop in 1973. In fact, the Crystal Cafe, Jimmie's Sandwiches, the Cervantes Restaurant, and local drug stores all sold Cuban sandwiches in Orlando in the 1930s. While Crespi undoubtedly revived the popularity of the sandwich there, the Cervantes had aggressively marketed Cuban sandwiches in Orlando with a *lonchero* facing the street for almost twenty years before closing in 1955.[39]

One origin story had the sandwich brought to Miami by José Miguel Gómez, a vocational educator in Cuba, in 1959. Upon arrival in Miami, Gomez resorted to washing dishes at El Toledo, one of the few Cuban restaurants in town at the time. He suggested that the owner add Cuban sandwiches to the menu, and Gómez became a *lonchero* overnight. He sold a hundred sandwiches on the first day at one dollar each. In several days, sales rose to five hundred daily. Then, reflecting on his own difficulties as an exile, Gómez created a smaller version that sold for sixty cents that became an instant success. About a year after featuring the sandwich, Gómez added Swiss cheese, reluctantly raising the price. The dishwasher-turned *lonchero* churned out sandwiches for the next three years.[40]

Back in Havana, vendors marketed the sandwich to different strata of society. In exile, the sandwich became much more equalized in price and quality. Raising prices for fellow exiles was too painful to bear.[41]

The Sandwich Temple

In 1967, at age thirty-one, Raúl Galindo found himself alone as a refugee in Chicago working as a packer in an electronics factory. As a man who always seemed to be brimming over with poetry, song, and a wicked sense of humor, it did not take long for Raul to stand out.

"After six months, I made Cuban sandwiches at home and took them to sell to my colleagues," he said. For his coworkers too poor to buy one, he gave them away. The packing job was merely a stepping-stone toward a new dream: opening his own restaurant.

Two decades before, Raúl got his first taste of the hospitality business in Cuba. In 1947, at age twelve, young Raul and his brother Luis, then twenty-six, moved from Matanzas to Havana with big dreams. When he took a job as a kitchen apprentice at the Royalty Cafeteria, which Luis had opened in Havana's La Víbora ward, it felt natural. At last, all six of the Galindo brothers, of whom Raúl was the youngest, worked in restaurants. No cafeteria in Havana could survive without serving good sandwiches. Raúl and Luis went on to open El Morro in central Havana.

The Galindo brothers lost their budding restaurant empire to the revolution and moved to the United States. Raúl escaped Cuba in 1967, worked a packing job in Chicago, and then settled in Miami four years later. He had $3.54 to his name when he arrived in the Magic City. He started working in a shoe store before taking a job as a *lonchero* at the Yayo Cafeteria, all the time with an eye toward opening his own eatery.

"The first step was to rent a small cafeteria in a Varadero supermarket," Galindo recalled. Then he found a property, a failed Arby's location, that he could purchase on Coral Way and Twenty-ninth Avenue. In 1974, a $68,000 loan was enough to launch the Latin American Cafeteria. The skills the brothers learned in Cuba became instrumental in their success. "When we arrived here from Cuba in 1962," Raúl said, "we saw that here in Miami at restaurants they used their hands to make sandwiches," rather than a *lonchero*'s blade. "These people had forgotten the way to do it. The style of Cuba." The *loncheros,* with their large knives and forks in perpetual motion, demonstrated the Latin American's commitment to cleanliness, Galindo claimed.

The Galindo brothers opened four more locations in the Miami area and inspired a generation of imitators, sometimes employing deceptive names such as the Latin American Cafe to lure in consumers. A little over a decade after receiving that first loan of $68,000, Galindo boasted that the cafeteria chain was valued at a cool two million dollars.[42]

Although the Versailles Restaurant was the political epicenter of exile Miami, the ultimate shrine to the Cuban sandwich was undoubtedly Galindo's original Latin American Cafeteria. "The three loncheros, as those who prepare the sandwiches are called," the *Miami Herald* noted, "do not stop cutting ham, cheese, pickles, bread. They look like knife jugglers. They require two bakeries for the Cuban and French breads they use daily."

Every week, the eatery served 1,800 pounds of ham, 1,700 pounds of pork, and 1,200 pounds of Swiss cheese on its sandwiches alone, including the one-pound special. Five *loncheros* worked the counter for sixty hours a week each, along with a full-time slicer to help supply them, selling about 1,400 sandwiches daily, half of them served through the walk-up window. The lonchero's blades took a toll on their butcher blocks, which had to be replaced every eighteen months or so.[43]

The volume was all the more impressive considering that there are only thirty-two seats around the bar and later, another forty under the umbrellas just outside. Although it was called a cafeteria and served a menu of hot Cuban dishes, the Latin American's horseshoe counter and old-school *loncheros* placed the sandwich in the center of the proceedings. Rather than sully the Cuban sandwich with additions and adaptations, Miami shops such as the Latin American created new combinations without calling them "Cuban" sandwiches. Only the classic warranted the "Cuban" moniker. Just as France has its "mother sauces," the Cubans have their mother sandwich of sorts. Galindo's menu eventually expanded to more than forty sandwich offerings.

The original Latin American Cafeteria on Coral Way elevated the sandwich to new heights. Miami Cuban sandwich enthusiast Dan Grech observed,

> A man behind a plexiglass divider crafted my sandwich. He wielded a two-foot-long serrated knife, long enough to cut down a tree. He split a loaf of Cuban bread, smeared a pat of room temperature butter, wiped the knife against his white apron, carved from a slab of dripping roast pork, wiped his knife, added slices of sweet ham and *queso suizo,* wiped, smeared yellow mustard, wipe, then expertly flipped a single pickle slice into the air.[44]

The *New York Times* wrote about the Cuban sandwich in 1989, featuring it in a story about newly emerging regional culinary favorites. The Latin American Cafeteria and the Galindo brothers deservedly took center stage:

> As served at the five Latin American cafeterias in Miami, each owned by one of the Galindo brothers, one sandwich is often enough for two people, and it still takes two fists to get a proper grip on a half. The secret of the sandwich, said Reinaldo Galindo, owner of the 27th avenue restaurant, is the curing and roasting of the meat.[45]

Perhaps the best ode to the *loncheros* at the Latin American was published in 2002 by the *New York Times.*

> The Latin American cafeteria is a former Arby's roast beef stand on Coral Way on the west side of Miami, ten minutes or so from downtown. It's nothing much to look at—just a bunch of plastic chairs and tables grouped

under an awning, plus a few more seats inside the restaurant proper. But no matter what the time of day, no matter what the season, the parking lot is jammed and excited eaters fill every place, chattering and gesturing with pure pleasure.

Peer inside the Latin American and watch a master at work. You will see an agile counter man wielding a broad-bladed, round ended knife. Stacked in front of him are thin hand cut slices of roasted leg of pork, Swiss cheese and a ham. When an order comes in—and the orders come in pretty much without interruption—he lays open a roll with his knife, quickly painted with margarine and piles on the fillings with abandon, as many as a half-dozen slices of each, using the knife as a spatula. Then he squeezes the two halves together with his hands and slaps it into a press. What emerges is slightly gooey and totally glorious: a perfect example of cheap, humdrum ingredients transformed into something spectacular.[46]

Much like Versailles, the Latin American has taken on a quasi-sacred status among exiles, not only for the food it serves but for its authenticity as an expression of *cubanidad* (loosely defined, "the Cuban condition," the essence of being Cuban). Galindo had succeeded in creating the illusion of Havana through its simple pleasures. Most importantly, one could go hours without hearing haughty English being spoken, but instead the melodious chatter of overlapping conversations and debates *en Español*. The *Nuevo Herald* set the scene:

> Every night, sometimes the later the better, there are many tables full of people who come to enjoy the breezes of Coral Way under the umbrellas. The waitresses can't cope, so if you're in a hurry don't go that night. Wait for a night with a clear sky when you can really enjoy the old Cuban music, which is heard through the speaker, and what it does to you. You feel that you are in Havana (if you close your eyes). A medianoche with a good mamey shake takes one back into the open air in front of the Capitol in Havana. When word gets out about the Coral Way's Latin American al fresco dining, it will soon be filled with "gringos" arriving on buses. Then you will no longer be able to enjoy the typical atmosphere. You have to take advantage of it while it lasts.[47]

Tampa may lay claim to historic precedent and quibble about salami or bread, but Miami exiles are too busy living their *cubanidad* out loud to care. For many, the greatest shrine to the Cuban sandwich is on Coral Way.

La Frita Cubana

All over Miami and much of the Cuban diaspora, griddles are sizzling with the *frita cubana,* another important sandwich to emerge from the Cuban Republic. Casual observers might see a hamburger with potato sticks thrown on top, but much like the Cuban sandwich, there is much more nuance than meets the eye. In old Cuba, street vendors prepared raw meatballs of ground beef, often mixed with pork and/or small amounts of chorizo or seasoned with the spices associated with it, especially paprika. When a customer ordered a *frita,* the vendor smashed a meatball onto his griddle. Seared and cooked quickly, the patty was served on a round Cuban bread–based bun.

Besides its seasoned flavor, the *frita's* textures are a sensational treat. In that respect, the secret weapon is the crispy shoestring potatoes mounded between the patty and the top bun. On the island, early Cuban vendors often used fried strands of malanga, a starchy root vegetable indigenous to Cuba, rather than potato. Today, lesser eateries may serve potato sticks straight out of the can, but hot, house-fried potato strings give far more nuance to the experience. Sometimes cooked with seasoned tomato sauce or topped with ketchup or *mojo,* the *frita* is much more than a burger and shoestring fries on a bun but instead another expression of Cuba's casual cuisine that has yet to be fully appreciated in Florida and beyond.

The pleasures of the *frita* were certainly appreciated in Cuba, where it found fans across society by the 1920s. "The Cuban frita," the *Nuevo Herald* noted, "the maximum exponent of fast food, [was typical] of the fast living and bad eating of the capital that was spreading across the island." By day, low-paid laborers could rely on cheap *fritas* for lunch, or those attending baseball games and other fiestas. After dark, theater-goers and nightclub revelers also relied on *fritas* for sustenance.[48]

Along with cheap beef, a similar cost-cutting measure was responsible for the amazing flavor of the potatoes. Cuban wine bars and emporiums bought canned Spanish and Cuban chorizo seasoned with Andalusian *pimentón* (paprika) that had been packed in fat. These businesses sold the cans, bereft of chorizo but still holding the prized fat, to the *frita* vendors. Too rich and pungent to serve alone, *frita* vendors added the chorizo's packing fat to their cooking grease. The resulting smell and taste of the fries, which were served separately or on a *frita,* were a signature scent from Havana's streets to its cinemas.[49]

The informality of Cuban culture and the *frita* itself is reflected by the fact that its greatest practitioner had no name, but a place. In old Havana, at the intersection of Zapata and Paseo in El Vedado, the temple of the *frita* resided. "And many nights, at the exit of the cinemas, long lines of cars were seen" to procure the best *fritas* and fries in town. No one did more to popularize the *frita* in Cuba than Sebastián Carro Seijido at Puerto de Sagua restaurant in the 1950s. Carro elevated the *frita* from a greasy, guilty pleasure to a national delicacy with quality ingredients and keen customer service.[50]

In 1961, Dagoberto Estevil opened Miami's first restaurant specializing in *fritas*. There are *frita* makers and then there is the king, Victoriano Benito González, who honed his skills at his brother's *frita* stand back in Placetas. They sold *fritas* until the Cuban regime shut down all private restaurants in 1968. In 1979, González founded El Rey de Las Fritas, whose name crowned him the king of *fritas,* which helped vault the sandwich into the national consciousness. Any trip to Miami is not complete without a *frita* and fruity *batido* shake.[51]

Perfecting the Ritual

Although forming any consensus beyond ousting Castro proved difficult in exile, the Cuban sandwich was fairly standardized in Miami after 1959, with an emphasis on size and value. Accordingly, the fillings would be streamlined. Ingredients such as mortadella/bologna, turkey, salchichón/salami would be abandoned, as they added to the sandwich's cost. Only ham and pork remained as the essential meats of the sandwich in exile. One could say the sandwich was democratized. In republican Havana, vendors specialized in serving certain strata of society, and their prices and locations often determined who dined there. Although people were free to dine where they liked, bricklayers and bankers rarely ate the same sandwich in Cuba. In Miami, sandwiches were far more homogeneous in quality and cost.

Since the best cafés prepared their own ham and pork roasts, the carving skill of the *lonchero* was paramount in creating a sandwich with thin slices that was pleasant to eat. His skills also determined the profit margin of the shop, since overly thick slices and more generous portions would cost the house more money. Paltry portions might lose his hungry clientele.

Besides preserving the *lonchero* institution, Miami added its own flourish that has become synonymous with the sandwich itself: pressing. To prepare warm sandwiches, the earliest *loncheros* used a hot tailor's iron as a makeshift press or toasted sandwiches in the oven. The electric sandwich press appeared in Cuba and the United States in the 1920s, and by the 1960s, it changed the shape of the hot Cuban sandwich forever. Miami's *loncheros* and cafés popularized the electric sandwich press like never before. Several sandwiches relied on presses to shape them, such as the "flying saucer." Miami's soft Cuban bread especially benefits from pressing, so for many, a hot sandwich became a necessity. The sandwich was always susceptible to being too large to comfortably bite. A couple minutes in the jaws of a hot press heats the sandwich and makes it easier to eat by compacting its contents and toasting the chewy Cuban bread. Cut diagonally, the sandwich presents two long points for ideal biting. As a hot sandwich built around hot fat and dry, crispy bread, raw vegetables such as onions, lettuce, and tomato only serve to water down the final product.

The *New York Times* observed,

> There are endless options of course. You can have your sandwich with or without mustard, with or without pickles. You can add a little pizzazz by ordering a Cubano with a few slices of chorizo added, and a lot more with the garlic citrus sauce called mojo. Once in awhile, a chef with attitude will substitute manchego or some other fancy cheese for plain old Swiss. Different sandwich joints cook their pork in different ways, which helps to account for the subtle differences in flavor from one place to the next. Some marinate the pork in lime juice before they roast it, for example. Others put lard or garlic in the pan. But the real aficionado will tolerate only so much messing around with the formula.[52]

For Cuban exiles in the United States, their cuisine became a pillar of identity and resistance against both the revolution and the pressure to fully Americanize. Cuban cuisine, and by extension the sandwich, was to be revered and preserved by the exiles, not trifled with.

Dennis Martínez Miranda,
Cubanidad 1885 (Las Vegas, Nevada)

A native of Cuba, Chef Dennis Martínez Miranda does not remember ever having eaten a Cuban sandwich on the island. "The first time I personally encountered and ate a Cuban sandwich was in Hialeah, Florida," he recalls. Since then, "I have eaten many sandwiches in Miami," he says. "Honestly, most weren't very good. I'm not sure if it's because of the quality of the components or because of a lack of attention. But still, when I had one for the first time, I fell in love with the mix of all the ingredients."

Born in Madruga, Cuba, Chef Dennis Martínez Miranda never saw a Cuban sandwich while growing up on the island. Today he runs a restaurant, Cubanidad 1885, that specializes in the sandwich in Las Vegas, Nevada. Courtesy of Cubanidad 1885.

Many sandwich practitioners prefer the meats cut into slightly thicker, more manageable slices and never sliced too thinly or shredded. At Cubanidad 1885 in Las Vegas, Nevada, Chef Dennis Martínez Miranda favors more substantial slices.

Born in Madruga, a small town in Cuba located in the eastern part of the Mayabeque province, between Matanzas and Güines, Dennis often tagged along with his mother, a professional cook. He developed a deep interest in Cuban cuisine from an early age. Later, when the family immigrated to Venezuela, they opened a small, family eatery. "Mami cooked, I cleaned up," Chef Dennis recalls. But soon Dennis was in charge of developing the menu, cooking, and creating new dishes. When his brother offered to pay his tuition to study cooking, he jumped at the chance, studying at the Marie-Antoine Carême Culinary Academy and later at Le Cordon Bleu Culinary Institute in Miami.

There in the Magic City, Chef Dennis sharpened his skills in local restaurants until he landed a job at Son Cubano, a stylish Cuban-Asian restaurant. Working alongside Chef Douglas Rodríguez, considered the *padrino* of Nuevo Latino Cuisine, he began participating in food events such as the South Beach Food and Wine Festival. Soon Chef Dennis's food, rich with the earthy, savory flavors of his native Cuba, was being celebrated. When two investors asked him to open a Cuban restaurant in Las Vegas, Chef Dennis eagerly accepted. Cubanidad 1885 was born.

The investors had lived for several years in Tampa, Florida, where they had become fond of Cuban food, often dining out in Ybor City. Taking 1885 from the year that the Tampa neighborhood was founded by cigar producers, they wanted to recreate some of the traditional dishes they warmly remembered. With their input, Chef Dennis created the menu, featuring what would become his best-selling items: two versions of the Cuban sandwich.

The "305" (a reference to the Miami area code) has roast pork, smoked ham, and Swiss cheese. The Original Ybor is described by Chef Dennis as being more traditional: roast pork, glazed ham, Genoa salami, and Swiss cheese. Both sandwiches have house-made pickle slices and a house-made mustard sauce that combines regular, Dijon, and grain mustard, plus a bit of mayonnaise, sour cream, and a touch of honey. Stacked on house-made Cuban bread (Chef Dennis finds authentic Cuban bread difficult to source in Las Vegas), the bread is brushed with a composite butter that is made with both garlic confit and fresh garlic. The requisite pressing on *la plancha* finishes the sandwich, cut deeply on the diagonal so that each half looks more like a triangle.

When asked if there are any versions of the sandwich that he cannot abide by, Chef Dennis says, "For me, at least sixty per cent of it is the roast pork—it's got to be marinated and have Cuban flavor. It cannot be dry; it must be juicy. The bread is also very important. It's got to be of high quality. It should toast up golden and crispy." He accedes that some versions with roast beef or pastrami can be delicious. "Change is okay. I love innovations, but the important thing is that what is *Cuban* about the sandwich is maintained—the taste of mojo, the Creole flavor—that is what I insist on."

This young chef has many plans for the future: new locations of Cubanidad 1885 will soon open, and he vows the restaurant will start making its own ham. In the meantime, he continues to dream and experiment, reflecting on what he calls his "100 percent Cuban identity" and what that means in his kitchen.

Carlos Argüelles,
The Cuban Sandwich Factory (Belfast, Ireland)

"La cocina para mi es cultura. Si no luchamos por eso, se muere," Carlos Argüelles plaintively argues from his Cuban Sandwich Factory restaurant in Belfast, Northern Ireland. As he recounts the many twists and turns of his immigrant journey from Cuba, to Ecuador, Scotland, Spain, and eventually Ireland, it is evident that this belief—"The kitchen for me is culture. If we don't fight for that, it will die."—directs his culinary passion and his work.

The oldest of seven siblings, Carlos learned to cook at his mother's side, a single mom in Matanzas, Cuba. While his mother was at work, five-year-old Carlos began cooking simple Cuban meals for his family. Although he later earned degrees in economics and chemistry, it would be the kitchen that would prove to be his best education and salvation.

As a young boy, Carlos would visit his *abuela* (grandmother) who lived in Oriente, on the other side of the island. Separated from Haiti by the narrow Windward Passage, Carlos's grandmother had grown up with Haitians and was a fervent believer and practitioner of *santería,* the syncretic Afro-Caribbean religion with Yoruba origins. Her words would be prophetic: "Carlos, remember that everything you ask for has consequences, so be careful what you ask for." Abuela's words continue to impact him today. "I wait for opportunity to come to me," he says, "if it comes, it comes. I have a lot of patience."

To hear Carlos's life story, it seems it has been one unplanned, fortuitous event after the other. He made a failed attempt to leave Cuba in 1993 on a raft (he was intercepted by Cuban authorities and put in jail). Shortly after, when Carlos helped a stranger who had missed his flight out of Cuba, he turned out to be an Ecuadorian businessman who would assist Carlos in leaving the island. That opportunity led to others, from the restaurant he set up in Ambato, Ecuador; to the casual meeting of his future (Irish) wife who was teaching English in Ecuador at the time; to his development as a chef at a series of culinary programs and restaurants in the United Kingdom; to the accidental discovery of a market in Belfast that would launch his career in the city.

He married his Irish love and settled in Belfast taking odd jobs as a chef. On his way home from work one day (as a cook in the field kitchen for *Game of Thrones,* which was filming in Northern Ireland), he chanced upon a market with kiosks selling produce, baked goods, and prepared foods. On a lark, he filled out an application to put up a kiosk of his own. As he contemplated the question—

What would you sell at this market?—without thinking, he wrote down "Cuban Sandwiches." Carlos submitted the application and promptly forgot about it until a few weeks later when he received a letter in the mail saying he was approved to set up a booth of his own.

As Carlos stared at the letter, he realized he had not had a Cuban sandwich for many years. "For a long time, I did not cook Cuban food because it would bring me too much nostalgia," he says. His first taste of a Cuban sandwich was on a train visiting his grandmother when he was a young boy. Although it was not toasted because the vendors did not have access to a *plancha* on the train, Carlos tried to conjure up the taste in his mind and on his palate. His memory, along with a bit of Internet research, yielded a working recipe.

For Carlos Argüelles, his journey from Cuba to Belfast, Ireland, was filled with struggle, romance, and the opportunity to come to terms with his own troubled history on the island of his birth. In this photo at his restaurant, the Cuban Sandwich Factory, he celebrates Cuban cuisine with Carmina Morales. Courtesy of Cuban Sandwich Factory.

Carlos's friends joked that he would be lucky if he sold twenty sandwiches on his first day; Carlos packed enough bread rolls to make forty. Almost as soon as he put a sign up on his kiosk and opened for business, a line began to form. Within twenty minutes, Carlos had sold out of all forty sandwiches, with people in line clamoring for more. Quickly buying bread from a nearby vendor, he kept making sandwiches until he exhausted his supplies. Week after week, the same scene repeated itself with an increasing number of sandwiches and happy customers.

Carlos's success led to two brick-and-mortar restaurants, with the market stand still in operation. Offers have come in to set up restaurants in London, China, Australia, and elsewhere. But both the COVID-19 pandemic and Carlos's own humility—"I am humble. I make do with what comes my way," he says—put the brakes on expansion. Still, he enjoys plenty of attention in his transplant hometown these days, holding court like the *loncheros* of yore:

> I decided to have an open kitchen (something that is taboo here). I wanted an open door, open policy—a show in front of the customers. The customer sees how the sandwich is made: the bread, the pork, ham, Swiss cheese, mustard, pickles, hot press, the cutting. . . . The pianist and the cook are the same: they are predestined to be forgotten, to die poor. Both are virtuosos, but no one actually *sees* them. People perceive the beauty of the music, the taste of the food—but they don't remember those who created the beauty, the taste. When they come to my restaurant, I want them to remember.

Although it is not easy finding authentic Cuban bread in Northern Ireland, Carlos has been able to contract a purveyor who creates a bread that is crunchy on the outside, soft on the inside, the closest Carlos has been able to find. Along with house-seasoned and roasted meats, the Cuban Sandwich Factory produces what has become the gold standard for Cubanos in the region. Today, Carlos is content to share his love of his native cuisine with those in Belfast and those visiting, with occasional trips to Cuba to visit his mother and ninety-eight-year-old grandmother. "When I've gone to Cuba," Carlos explains, "I've returned recharged—it brings balance to my kitchen and to my cooking because sometimes I introduce too much British influence into my food." As diners tuck into plates of savory *ropa vieja*, sweet *platanitos*, and the iconic *sandwich cubano*, it is clear that Carlos's Cuban Sandwich Factory is not just a reflection of his culinary prowess, but a testament to his culture and his history.

6

Feast and Famine

The Boatlift

In the 1970s, Cuba coped with a generation of young, disaffected citizens unfulfilled by the roles that had been assigned to them by the state. An uneasiness pervaded the revolution until a crisis that began when unhappy citizens sheltered in the Peruvian embassy in a bid to leave. Castro exploited events to offload his most disillusioned citizens, criminals, and the mentally ill. Over a six-and-a half-month period beginning on April 15, 1980, about 125,000 fled in an improvised boatlift organized by private vessels from the United States. At the port of Mariel, where thousands of émigrés often waited days or weeks to gain passage to the United States, the Cuban government gouged desperate people ten dollars for ham sandwiches.[1]

When new Cuban arrivals (often referred to as *Marielitos*) poured into the Miami area, sympathizers donated countless Cuban sandwiches that would become the first bites of food many of the refugees ate in the United States. Here was the totem of exile, the heart and soul of the Cuban immigrant experience, a beacon of liberty and sustenance. As a new arrival from Mariel, Mercedes Hernández Martínez had survived a gauntlet of hostility on her way out of the country. She soon found herself holding a Cuban sandwich at Versailles, but she remained haunted by the young daughter she left behind. The child's grandmother would not hear of letting the four-month-old join Mercedes for the journey. For many new arrivals, even a hot sandwich was cold comfort.[2]

The new deluge of Cuban immigration underscored that Miami had permanently and radically changed from its sleepy old days. The Democratic Party, which once dominated Miami's elections, found its power eroded by growing Republican support, especially among the exiles. The Jewish "condo districts" had been challenged by the growing Cuban vote. Latin voters had a higher voter participation rate than Miami's more settled communities, but were still a minority. Burger King's Vice President David Talty and caterer Sara Sharpe opened The Lunch Basket in the Columbus Hotel Mall, where they exclusively served "American food" for people who would "turn green if they see one more Cuban sandwich," said Sharpe.[3]

After Mariel, the ire of some white voters fueled an "English only" law campaign that passed, rendering all government services available exclusively in English. Because of changing demographics, such a bill could not pass for long. Proponents of the bill said that the Cubans should become Americans by adopting English as a second language, and many did. Some Cuban-Americans protested the "emotional outburst" of other voters by lunching publicly on Cuban sandwiches while playing salsa on the radio. At the time, about one-third of Miami's 1.7 million residents spoke Spanish as a first language.[4]

The *Miami Herald* extolled the Cuban sandwich as cultural common ground and a possible way to bridge between Spanish- and English-speaking Miami.

> Pay attention now, all you folks who voted for the anti-bilingualism referendum. You are about to read how to make a proper Cuban sandwich, and if you haven't noticed, a lot more of them are selling in restaurants than the all-American hot dog. In the better places around, it is made from a whole baked ham and a freshly roasted pork shoulder. Nothing frozen, pressed, packaged or mass-produced. One of the best places to observe the care and feeding of Cuban sandwiches to the multitudes is the Latin American Cafeteria, where every sandwich is made in a sort of bull ring—a *plaza de sandwich* surrounded by counter and stools.[5]
>
> As a people in exile, Cuban Americans of all classes cling to their gastronomic traditions. For many who were actually born in little Havana and have since moved away, the thirty block-long neighborhood strung out along southwest Eighth Street hasn't really changed much, at least in smell and flavor, since their youth. What's more, the restaurants there have not anglicized their cooking.[6]

Contradictions

In a sure sign of the Cubano's popularity, Miami's Continental National Bank sponsored a contest to identify the best in 1979. Several prominent competitors employed showmanship to sway the judges, using fancy blade work and one even using a maraschino cherry as garnish. Out of seven finalists, the four journalist judges, three being Cuban, chose a unanimous winner: Ricardo Pérez of the obscure La Arcada, while second place went to Eduardo Gómez of Los Pegaditos. Most of Miami's best sandwich shops did not bother to show up for reasons that will be discussed later. After the contest, the *Herald* concluded,[7]

> It may have become Americanized with yellow mustard and processed Swiss cheese in our constantly simmering melting pot, but the Cuban sandwich must be acknowledged as our most widely recognized ethnic food. Thin crusted, crackling Cuban bread is cut in half lengthwise, dabbed with butter and mustard, layered with ham, pork and cheese, dotted with a few slivers of sour pickle and slapped into a hot grill until it is flat, crisp and warm. There were some very well-known restaurants competing for the title of the best. They finished way down the list, despite efforts to impress the panel of judges with showmanship. The winner won simply because he used good quality baked ham from the butt, fresh roasted pork to carve and he took time enough to make sure a sandwich was fully grilled and hot inside. The losers used pre-sliced ham and pork more like luncheon meats, and served up sandwiches which were cold in the middle. The winner was awarded a free vacation trip in Mexico. The losers, many of whom did not take defeat gracefully, were left licking their wounds with mustard and pickle and vowing to return next year.[8]

By the time the Cuban sandwich became a recognized and revered tradition, the real thing was already fading fast. That is because the original Cuban sandwich was not a single recipe but a combination of handmade products. Not every innovation in sandwich making actually produced a better result. Besides inferior bread, two developments cheapened the *mixtos* of old: First, the replacement of *loncheros* with deli slicers, and second, the disappearance of handmade hams and roasts in favor of industrial lunchmeat loaves. These effort-saving innovations made it much easier for any grocery or gas station to prepare and serve their own estimation of the Cuban but quality suffered. It isn't especially difficult to assemble the ingredients to make a passable sandwich. Most are content to serve or eat a lunchmeat sandwich and call it a Cuban. Faced with a marketplace that had given up on quality, discerning consumers stopped looking for the best Cuban in favor of the cheapest.[9]

All kinds of food products are susceptible to the same economic forces (e.g., hamburgers, hot dogs, and pizza). Yet the struggle to preserve a worthy sandwich at a fair price could also help one understand the Cuban experience as a whole. Scholars of Cuban history have called it an "elusive nation caught between ideals and deep dissatisfaction." Time and again, the promise of Cuba has been frustrated from within and without, and the dream of a united, prosperous homeland gone unfulfilled. Cuban pride and cultural pessimism are baked into political sensibilities on both sides of the Florida Straits. A similar tension permeates the Cuban sandwich. With so many variables, a version built on consensus may be an impossible feat. In addition, the sandwich has been caught between equally high expectations of value and quality.[10]

It is helpful to remember that early versions of the sandwich originated in Havana as an urbane, expensive indulgence that required imported ingredients. New businesses marketed more affordable versions to the masses over time. Later, consumer demand fixed prices to unrealistically low levels, which eroded the quality of sandwiches everywhere. Along with the flavor, the novelty of the sandwich had worn off. A reporter for the *Palatka Daily News* (Florida) described the state of the Cuban sandwich in the 1970s.

> Like any great craft form, it [the Cuban sandwich] proliferated. It evolved, like Key lime pie, into a gastronomical treasure of our state. All of which brings us to the present, which in comparison to a past of flavorsome memory, can be a nasty jolt. Two chunks of soggy bread, garnished with mustard, holding a couple slices of slimy ham and two pieces of pickle of bright sea green hue, had been wrapped in film and tossed into the refrigerator case of a convenience store. The cost: 89 cents; The label: Cuban sandwich.[11]

During the 1970s and 1980s, both the *Tampa Tribune* and the *Miami Herald* held Cuban sandwich contests to find the best in their communities. While the winners all offered worthy entries, the overall quality of the sandwiches over the years revealed a market that was racing to the bottom in terms of quality. Just what comprised a Cubano was a source of constant debate among Tampa's judges. Restaurateur and contest judge Malio Iavarone insisted to a fellow judge, "There is no 'original' Cuban sandwich, you know that. There's no such thing." Jimmy Font, owner of the Alvarez Restaurant, said, "It's amazing how many people interpret the Cuban sandwich differently. It was always Cuban bread, a slice of ham, a slice of cheese, pickles and butter and that's it. There are other places that put on pork, salami, and turkey, which is not part of the Cuban sandwich. Lettuce and tomato and mayonnaise and mustard . . . why, I laugh. I don't know what kind of sandwich they're selling."[12]

Miami's 1979 Cuban sandwich contest mentioned above was one of the first critical discussions of the sandwich recorded in print. An event meant to celebrate the sandwich also pointed out the shortcomings of inferior specimens for the first time. Some of the losing contestants were critical of the entire process. At the time, it took a courageous and idealistic person to organize such an event in Miami. The story of Bernardo Benes is instructive here. A genuine leader in business and philanthropy, Benes supported a wide variety of humanitarian causes in Miami, advocating various assistance programs for the exile community and beyond. Benes was so sensitive to the needs of the people because he himself was an exile.[13]

In 1960, Benes began his new life with about two hundred dollars and a job as a janitor at a Miami bank. Seventeen years later, he and a partner established the Continental National Bank of Miami. His rise in the world of business and finance coincided with an almost ceaseless campaign, part philanthropic and part public relations, for Miami's growing exile community. For example, he founded a snack and sandwich bar that fed about one hundred thousand young "Pedro Pan" exiles at the Opa-Locka Airport over two years. Still, for various reasons, perhaps his Jewish faith or his father's Russian ancestry, many Cubans did not fully accept Benes as one of their own.[14]

Benes began his Miami experience as a militant exile who changed his views gradually. He observed that an adversarial approach had only further entrenched Castro's regime. Benes was keen to see Cubans take their destinies into their own hands by opening a dialogue. Simple but vital agreements might allow for exiles to visit family on the island again and send them financial assistance. If exiles could visit their mother's graves, he reasoned, his efforts would have been worthwhile.

Benes's first meeting with Castro took place in 1978 with the approval of President Jimmy Carter's administration. In one of his first visits, Benes and other émigrés flocked to the classic restaurant El Carmelo to indulge in the sandwiches, steaks, and ice cream they remembered. They found the chic emporium of old had degraded into a bleak dive with awful food. The mainstays of the old menu had been replaced by fish croquettes and sausage sandwiches, which Benes found inedible despite being very hungry.[15]

Successful negotiations enabled him to return to Miami with freed political prisoners, eventually leading to the release of 3,600. However, his high profile in the affair did not draw praise but scorn. Many of the most vocal Cubans in Miami violently disagreed with any dialogue between the exile community and the Cuban state. An infamous photo of Benes smoking a cigar with Castro was all they needed to see. Thereafter, the exile community, or at least the most vocal part of it, had marked Benes for excommunication from the exile community or even death.[16]

When his bank sponsored the Cuban sandwich contest in 1979, Benes was already notorious for his group's ongoing negotiations with Castro. Many potential participants and observers would have been repelled by the involvement of Benes and his bank. Still, he flirted with running for mayor of Miami in 1982. He often wore a bulletproof vest and survived at least one attempt on his life. In 1983, the militant exile group Omega 7 bombed the Continental National Bank, where he was still employed as vice president. Benes stepped down from his position to save the bank from further incidents. In the end, he was a pariah, banished from the exile community he had tried to help. After struggling to find steady work for many years, Raúl Galindo of the Latin America Cafeteria, the exile temple of the sandwich, hired Benes as a financial consultant in 1996. When the exile newspaper *Viva Semanal* wrote a scathing article mocking Benes, he was asked not to return to work. Even twenty years after starting the dialogue, Benes was still very much banished from Miami. For better or worse, Benes can be remembered as someone who started new conversations and fierce debate, not only about Cuba but also the sandwich that bears its name.[17]

Benes never held another Cuban sandwich contest, and no one in Miami saw the need to hold one. By the end of the 1980s, even the *Tampa Tribune* had lost the stomach for their annual Cuban sandwich competitions.

Miami's Cuban community gave rise to a wealth of cuisine, but much of the scene seemed to be stuck in time. The main players and the menu had not changed much, only narrowed. Accordingly, the *New York Times'* suggestions from 1991 could have applied from the mid-1970s until the 2010s: Versailles, La Esquina de Tejas (Cuban home cooking), Centro Vasco (elegant and more Spanish), and La Carreta (late night, 24 hour).[18]

The sandwich in Miami was never uniform. In a 1988 article about the Cuban sandwich, the *Miami Herald* noted the controversy surrounding the exact recipe. Some places employed French bread instead of Cuban. An informal survey found widely varying use of condiments, some electing to omit pickles, mustard, and mayonnaise altogether. Some added *mojo* sauce to their sandwiches. All of the sandwich vendors expressed a willingness to please their customers, but salami, lettuce, and tomato were not mentioned at all.[19]

Miami's Latinos—not just the Cuban Americans, but those of Colombian, Venezuelan and Argentine origin as well—have a purple passion for these succulent sandwiches. They're on sale all over town. Pizza parlors sell them. So do cafes, supermarkets and even the local outlets at McDonald's. People here eat Cubanos all day long, but especially at the end of the day. Inveterate night owls, the Latinos finish a session on the town with a sandwich.[20]

For all its popularity, the sandwich might lose its edge and become a shadow of a flavor all but forgotten, the mirage of a delicacy that dissolved upon one's approach. Despite the culinary crimes committed against it, the Cuban sandwich has survived the twentieth century—but what of the twenty-first? Tampa and Miami ultimately share the same heritage and face the same all-powerful enemy: mediocrity.[21]

Of Communism and Commerce

Over time, the exile community was able to arrive at a public consensus on several issues. A justified hatred of Castro and his regime would serve as the first tenet of exile. Second, Cuban exile cuisine was not negotiable. As the sandwich rose in popularity and became identified with Miami's exiles after 1959, it was also profoundly shaped by the exile experience.

With one voice, the exile community had denounced any dialogue with Castro's regime. Many exiles felt betrayed when President Jimmy Carter authorized travel between the two countries, as money from tourists and exiles would only aid the revolution. Still, the desire to see family and old haunts proved to be impossible to resist. Shortly after the change in policy, the Immigration and Naturalization Service quickly ran out of the forms required to visit Cuba. In all, about 150,000 exiles jumped at the chance to return to the island and visit family between 1979 and 1982, when President Reagan discontinued travel to Cuba.[22]

For all of the joy they brought, first encounters between the Cubans and visiting exiles often proved to be awkward. Family members who could visit for the first time found that more than ninety miles and twenty years separated them. Castro and the revolution had vilified exiles for a generation, calling them *gusanos*. The returning exiles had spent just as long convincing themselves that their families hated Castro as much as they did. Instead, visitors often found Cubans defending the state, noting the deep pride, public and private, that many citizens displayed for the revolution.[23]

On the other hand, the Cubans had heard many stories of the evils of capitalism and were surprised by the apparent wealth of the returning exiles. Invariably, the visitors arrived with armfuls of gifts for their relatives, which soon wrought havoc on their revolutionary spirit. Perceptive exiles might have had the forethought to pack a few sandwiches from Miami to give their families a taste of old Cuba, because the cuisine they once savored on the island had been relegated to its decadent past. The communist regime blanched at the flood of clothing, luxury foods, and other consumer goods, which provoked many Cubans to question its policies and priorities.[24]

Those exiles decrying the quality of sandwiches in the United States could still count many blessings. They lived and ate without the onerous restrictions imposed by Communist regulations and the equally pervasive US embargo. When the Cuban economy finally began to improve slightly in the mid-1970s, the state remained focused on subsistence. Consumer goods were almost nonexistent, but then so was the budget of the average worker. Most of Cuba's poor, who had stayed through the revolution, would live by and for the state. Only the black market (an entire subeconomy endemic to communist states) and remittances from abroad provided goods and income outside of the rigid state apparatus.[25]

Although the Cuban government stigmatized *gusanos* (worms) in the early years of the revolution, it later changed its tune, tolerating the presence of returning exiles as "dollar-bringers." For better or worse, travel to Cuba threw Castro's regime an economic lifeline.[26]

Even in the flush times of financial aid from the Soviet Union, Cuba was barely able to feed its population. Those visiting Cuba since the revolution have derided the poor quality and quantity of the food there. While shortages ruined home cooking in Cuba, gross government mismanagement undermined the restaurants that were meant to be "safety valves" for those frustrated by rationing. The National Institute of Tourist Industries, which once ran the bulk of eateries, displayed its hollow slogans on welcome mats, "My work is you," and "Your right is to enjoy; our duty is to serve."[27]

Exiles returning to visit relatives found their land practically barren of decent victuals. The mixed sandwiches of old seemed to have disappeared in favor of horrific farces posing as pizzas. Exile Enrique Fernández visited the island several times and was always "appalled" by the food. "Everything I remembered from my childhood had disappeared. It was at that moment that any solidarity I felt with the revolution left me. A system that couldn't make an edible pizza was just no damn good."[28]

The "Special Period"

In 1992, George Díaz returned to Cuba more than thirty years after he left at the age of four. "Returning home was wonderful, and it was horrible. I laughed with four second-cousins I had never met as they took me sightseeing through the city streets one afternoon, pausing to drink beers and eat a Cuban sandwich at a restaurant adjacent to the Cathedral Square in Havana. 'What a great sandwich,' one of them said, not knowing the pleasure of eating a *real* Cuban sandwich at the Latin American Cafeteria in Miami."[29]

Long before the "Special Period in Times of Peace," as the Castro regime called Cuba's post-Soviet crisis, its people had dealt with shortages. When the Soviet Union collapsed in 1991, most of its client states quickly joined the Western World's markets. Unable to stomach capitalism and unwilling to seek genuine rapprochement with the United States, Cuba and North Korea chose to defiantly buck the tides of history. While both communist regimes survived their "special period," some of their people were not so lucky. In Cuba, the revolution demanded the people undergo wartime austerity measures for a "Special Period." Transportation and agriculture collapsed on the island due to a fuel shortage. Restricted from purchasing oil or selling its sugar crop due to the US-led trade embargo, the Cuban economy seized up.

The nation's fortunes from republic to revolution can be traced through the lessons of Nitza Villapol, the most popular chronicler of Cuban cuisine. She began her television show in 1948, cooking quick and very simple *criollo* food. Published in 1954, one of her landmark cookbooks (which she updated all of her life), *Cocina al Minuto* (Minute Kitchen), is an exercise in capitalism. With its numerous ads and the placement of the advertised products directly in the recipes, the tome was designed to be profitable.

As the daughter of a Communist father who gave her a Russian name after being inspired by the revolution there, Villapol greeted Castro with open arms. After Castro took power, she continued her show on Cuba's state-run television and educated Cubans on how to conserve food. Shortages forced her to cut the chapter of her book devoted to sandwiches and snacks, as if those dearly beloved Cuban specialties no longer existed. While the volume of food increased for many Cubans under rationing, the people maintained unhealthy eating habits much like their counterparts in the United States.

Despite years of government propaganda and Villapol's own entreaties to eat a balanced diet, Cubans did not respond to the message. This was apparent in the 1970s when a scholar in the United States observed,

The Cuban diet is almost entirely contrary to good health and the Cuban climate. Fruits and vegetables are disdained; fish is looked down upon as something to be eaten when beef, pork, and chicken are not available; refined sugar (which is the mainstay of the Cuban economy) is dumped on everything to such an extent that it is probably slowly sapping the people of their energy and their health. If a Cuban has sweetened canned orange juice for breakfast, he typically adds two to five spoons of sugar. Rice is almost worthless when polished, as it is in Cuba. And so it goes. A detrimental diet coupled with almost universal cigarette consumption.[30]

While Villapol never lost patience with Cuba's lack of ingredients, she was privately disappointed in her nation of uncooperative pupils. In a rare personal interview toward the end of her life, Villapol came across as embittered.

I have tried for thirty years to change the Cuban diet. Cubans ruin their eating. I don't give a damn. All they want is pork, fried bananas and rice. You don't need meat to be well fed. What the hell do I care about rice? They're too finicky about what they eat.[31]

Villapol seemed so stoic because she was not a "foodie" at all. Educated in home economics, she got her start teaching people how to make do while rationing during World War II. According to those who knew her best, she did not enjoy cooking or eating especially, but teaching. Although Villapol would be condemned by the exiles for her compliance with Communism, her books are still like bibles of modern Cuban cuisine, and many worn copies adorn the most conservative kitchens of Miami. Although Villapol inspires nostalgia in many, she also has her detractors. Even many Cubans on the island blamed Villapol for the decline in Cuban cuisine. Exiles could console themselves that she never made a cent from sales in the United States. The predicament of disliking a person so closely identified with your beloved cuisine is just one of the conundrums of exile.[32] As much as she was enamored with Castro's revolution, she might have changed her mind if she had faced the same rigors as other Cubans. "I won't stand in line for any food," she said defiantly.[33]

Some Cuban citizens mourned the loss of their food culture to Communism and mass production. Government-run restaurants offered low quality food and bad service for high prices. "You generally know that you just walked into a government restaurant when you realize that no one cares you're there," a blogging tourist quipped. As if the Sovietization of Cuban culture wasn't bad enough, the shortages of the 1990s were the "coup de grace to popular food culture," Yenisel

Rodriguez wrote, "Free enterprise hasn't managed to create an authentic service culture, contenting itself with a rustic economic rationality that ends up disdaining the consumer much like the State does."[34]

As in the Soviet Union, Cuba's economy atrophied and went underground in the midst of systemic bottlenecks, complacency, and widespread theft among workers at state enterprises. Food production dropped by 40 percent between 1990 and 1994.[35] The cattle population plummeted as Cubans devoured the once-plentiful animals, or they died from hunger due to lack of feed. In response, the government instituted harsh penalties for killing or eating cows, worse penalties than for murder. Even stray cats and the animals in the Havana Zoo began to disappear.[36]

Thirty years after the fall of the USSR, food shortages in Cuba were still constant and ever shifting. Castro predicted that food rationing would end in 1965, but the system, symbolized by the ubiquitous *libreta* (state-issued ration book), still remained in place years after his death in 2016.[37] The quality of the available food certainly brought no honor to the revolution. The *Havana Times* reported, "Today, the menus at Cuba's state food industry establishments are a litany of super-greasy processed cold meats, extremely salty minced meats, snacks fried in saturated oils that are several days old, soft drinks and rancid sandwiches."[38]

The Cuban state began importing powdered cheese to take the place of the real thing in school menus, suggesting cafeterias use it as a pizza topping, which goes a long way toward explaining how pizza became so terrible under the state's culinary supervision. Since the early 1990s, frozen mystery-meat *croquetas* had become a cheap mainstay for snacks and meals. "People kid about croquettes that stick to your gums," the *Havana Times* recorded, "that stretch like chewing gum, the ones that can crack people's teeth, explosive croquetas, or 'conundrum croquettes' (with indistinguishable flavors)." *Croquetas* are so popular and affordable that they too have run short. The *croqueta* sandwich has become another common symbol of scarcity. And as a food of last resort, people lacking funds ate *pan con mayonesa,* a pressed mayo sandwich, among the cheapest morsels on the island.[39]

In her novel *Ruins,* Achy Obejas wrote of a character named Rosita who must sell sandwiches to survive the US embargo. Using a "blanket normally used for mopping floors which [she] had beaten and marinated in spices and a little beef broth, the texture of the wool had been transformed into what they all imagined steak was like, something tender and chewy. The success of her enterprise had come as much from her ingenuity as from the tricks memory plays." It didn't matter much that Rosita could not find beef since no one remembered what it tasted like anyway.[40]

New hotels for foreign tourists provided muted opportunities to the common people. Foreign investors leased Cuban labor for $1,500 monthly to build their hotels, of which the worker received $10, plus a bologna sandwich and soft drink daily for lunch. Still short of cash, most of the workers sold their state-issued sandwiches for a dollar, netting an extra $30 salary each month. Canned hams were offered for workers who didn't miss any work for a month, providing an incentive where wages could not.[41]

Attracting tourists became part of a strategy to obtain Western currency in the face of the continuing US embargo. But Cuba lacked culinary attractions. In 1993, the state allowed *paladares,* or restaurants in private homes, with a maximum of twelve seats, to fill the gap. Still, the state reserved premium ingredients such as beef or shrimp for its own enterprises, forcing some *paladares* to resort to black market products.

A Cuban named Armando ran a *paladar* out of his home for several years without incident. When the government opened a sandwich stand two doors down, the health inspectors came all the time and soon put him out of business by a thousand cuts, minor infractions such as cooking while wearing a wedding band.[42] "They put you out of business, and then you're forced to work for their restaurant making the state wage of 200 pesos a month, right next door." Every private business operated at the mercy of the inspectors, who wielded a great deal of "arbitrary power." In 2011, the government allowed private restaurants with up to fifty seats, another uncomfortable step toward a free market.[43]

Some Cubans augmented their incomes through less-acceptable methods such as dating tourists. Pico Iyer reported "the tourist hotels are filled with Cuban teenagers reddening their lips with children's crayons." Teenage girls clustered around the entrances to the dance clubs, hoping a tourist would pay their three-dollar cover charge, in the land where doctors made $20 a month.[44]

When *Food and Wine* asked Ivan Justo, Fidel Castro's former private chef, for dining suggestions in 2017, he included upscale destinations where one would be more likely to nosh on enchiladas, kebabs, "eggplant caviar," ceviche, and honey-mustard chicken than anything Cuban. For those in search of Cuban flavors, *croquetas,* roast pork, and the ubiquitous beans and rice would have to suffice. The depleted Cuban larder made an embarrassment of the people's culinary heritage, which would not be celebrated by its citizens or Western tourists. Soybeans became especially maligned by the Cubans who were compelled to eat them.[45]

Daniel Figueredo and Rosa Romero, Sanguich de Miami (Miami)

As much as Rosa Romero loved Cuban sandwiches, she found ordering one to her specific tastes was a minefield. "My entire life, ordering was a little bit of a nightmare. 'Oh, here she goes,' the women or the men at the window, or wherever we were, always seemed annoyed by my requests. Even with all its imperfections, it's a sandwich I loved."

"Even when it was mediocre at best," her husband Daniel Figueredo interjected.

Born and raised in the Miami area, Rosa was the child of *Marielitos*. In 2014, when she met her husband Daniel, her love of Cuban sandwiches intensified. During their frequent sandwich outings by night, Rosa always ordered a medianoche, while Daniel invariably ordered the Miami sandwich, a sort of turkey and bacon club on Cuban bread, favoring Sergio's or La Carreta. There is nothing more Cuban than Daniel's "game-changer" tip to dip one's sandwich in hot cafe con leche.

Born in Chicago with an artistic eye, Daniel Figueredo had a fast-paced career in textile engineering, fashion, branding, design, and architecture. In a crushing setback, the recession of 2008 forced him to close his fashion business and start over. He met Rosa while designing and building stores for other companies. She worked in litigation as an executive paralegal for many years. As successful as they were on paper, they both felt trapped by their high-performing careers.

Daniel took vital marketing lessons away from his experiences. "It's no longer creative," he says of modern branding, "It's a science." He was eager to apply the principles he learned to his own new concept. He had long harbored a secret business plan for a gourmet sandwich shop concept.

While Rosa agreed to start the business, she suggested a crucial change in direction, perhaps thinking of her own sandwich experiences in Miami. "I told him, think about the best Cuban sandwich in Miami. You have to really think about it because it's all the same. They're buying French's mustard, jarred pickles, *jamón de agua* [Rosa mocks the cheap, water-logged boiled ham favored by the cheapest places], and Swiss cheese that never quite melts. It grew to be a low-quality sandwich that was fast and easy to get, you knew what you were going to get no matter where you sat to eat it, and it was a filler. I think Miami really needs a good Cuban sandwich shop. Besides the Versailles and La Carretas of the world, what else comes to mind? It's all the same thing."

At that moment, the stars aligned and Daniel had an epiphany. They wouldn't simply add Cuban sandwiches to their menu but build the entire concept around

Rosa Romero and Daniel Figueredo left the corporate world to perfect several varieties of Cuban sandwiches at Sanguich de Miami. With their house-made ingredients, they seek to elevate the sandwich without compromising its identity. Courtesy of Sanguich.

them. Everything fell into place after that. While they still worked their jobs, they cut corners and saved every penny with an eye on their sandwich dream.

They considered *La Republica de Pan* (The Republic of Bread) as their company name when a good friend suggested simply calling it *Sanguich,* a common Cuban pronunciation that instantly communicates who they are and the sandwiches they sell. It was also a word that anyone in Miami could deeply identify with in a light-hearted way. For Cubans, exiles, and Cubanophiles, that single word establishes an immediate emotional connection.

They decided to launch Sanguich at the Coconut Grove Art Festival, a large annual three-day event that attracted 250,000 visitors. They prepped 750 pounds of *lechón* using a special recipe they had developed. A family friend, owner of the Cuba Bakery in Homestead, agreed to roast and store the pork in his walk-in cooler.

The arts festival was a triumph for their budding brand, not just because of the huge lines of customers they served but in Daniel's story of winning over an imperious Cuban *abuela,* about seventy years old. "It looked like a line for miles, and I couldn't look up."

When the woman cut in front of everyone in the long line "like they didn't even exist," she demanded to know what Daniel was selling. When he explained that they were selling *lechón* sandwiches with plantain chips and a dipping sauce for twelve dollars, she frowned. "This is disrespectful!" she groused in Spanish. "Besides, no one can make better *pan con lechón* than me!"

He defended his prices and his pork, insisting it was indeed the best in Miami. Then, with no regard for the masses waiting in line behind her, she grudgingly demanded a sandwich and handed over her money.

The rest of the day was a blur of making sandwiches and taking cash, but at some point, the grouchy *abuela* returned with a much friendlier disposition. "*Mi'jito,*" she said, much more softly than she spoke before. "I'm so sorry. That was the best *pan con lechón* I ever had."

Daniel recalled, "It was at that moment I looked at Rosa and said, 'I think we have something!'"

After that first festival, a large event being held two weeks later, the Carnival on the Mile, invited Sanguich to join the event's vendors. They sold out in four hours. Encouraged by their success, Daniel signed up for the Cuban Sandwich Smackdown, an event founded in Tampa that was visiting Miami in 2017, forcing them to consider the ham they would serve. They resolved to make their own superior ham in the six weeks before the contest.

"We went into a market saturated with the product already, as it is here in Miami," Daniel observed. "We truly needed to do something that was going to set us apart from the rest. Cultivating a new generation of Cuban sandwiches had to be at the top of our list. Something new that still represented the classic, the authenticity of what the Cuban sandwich represents to our culture, but reviving it where you don't compromise what it is. Whatever we did had to be authentic. The look, the feeling, the taste, the sound, the people, the language, if it wasn't authentic, it wasn't going to resonate with me."

Since they found the available commercial bread to be lacking, they developed their own, both Cuban bread and medianoche bread, opting for sandwich-sized rolls rather than the yard-long loaves of old, giving each sandwich crusty ends. "I always felt like I was sharing my sandwich with two other people," Daniel said.

Daniel understands why the pickles and mustard can be an acquired taste. "The Germans used pickles and mustard to accentuate the meats. When you put pickles and mustard together it does a disservice to the meat and there's too much vinegar, which is why people don't like mustard and pickles. We never put them together."

The couple resolved to create their own pickles and, at Rosa's insistence, mustard.

"Everybody fought me on making our own mustard. It's a twenty-day process, completely worth it. People are too worried about the money aspect of it: 'I'm just trying to turn my sandwich and make three, four dollars, and how do we do that quickly and cheaply?' That's not our motivation. How do we put out the best Cuban sandwich with the best ingredients that best represents our tradition that doesn't compromise who we are?"

Sanguich applies condiments judiciously to allow customers to fully taste the house-made meats. They also use overlapping ingredients to flavor the meats and the condiments so they reinforce rather than clash with one another. The mustard and pork share ingredients as well as the pickles and the ham. Before pressing, they brush their sandwiches with lard rendered from their ham and *lechón*. "When you bite our sandwich, you never taste the mustard, the pickles, the ham, or the *lechón*." Instead, all the ingredients harmonize into one united flavor that rules them all.

To minimize costs and keep overhead low, they used a shipping container as their first home, which Daniel built out into a chic "luxury restaurant" in Little Havana. Shortly after opening in September 2017, the *Miami New Times* featured Sanguich in a laudatory review, which served notice that a new sandwich contender had arrived in Miami. People caught on fast, and Sanguich began appearing on top ten Cuban sandwich lists.

Just as business was humming, a change in political guard resulted in the City of Miami shutting down Sanguich in February 2018, just four months after opening. The city advised that they could reopen if the container was made a mobile business on wheels. After Sanguich complied at considerable expense, the city changed its mind and denied approval to reopen. Since the city wouldn't recognize the container as a mobile or a permanent structure, they had essentially banished Sanguich from the world of business with no recourse available to the eatery. Some speculated that innovative businesses in Little Havana were being harassed to protect the area's older, more influential establishments.

Amid a groundswell of support from the community, for months the couple fought against the city's unfair treatment to no avail. Daniel defiantly promised the city commissioners that Sanguich would not leave Little Havana. Eventually,

Daniel Figueredo and Rosa Romero at Sanguich de Miami, the challenge was to make a high-quality product that stayed true to its roots. Courtesy of Sanguich.

he concluded they did not have the influence to win against the city's capricious policies on mobile/container businesses, nor could he find alternate locations.

"We just wanted to sell sandwiches," Rosa said. "It had become so difficult at that time to do something that was so simple." Rosa applied for food stamps and Medicare for the children. She told Daniel if Sanguich was not open and running by the time the benefits ran out six months later, she would go back to work to provide for their family, which now included two children.

Determined to maintain Sanguich's clientele, Daniel built out a brick-and-mortar location nearby with whatever funds they could muster. After four months of desperate labor and expense, they opened Sanguich de Miami's first restaurant in August 2018, the same month that their government benefits expired. At 734 square feet, it wasn't much bigger than the container, but it was all they needed. They were so concerned about the city undermining their efforts that they did not go public as Sanguich until after all their permits were in place.

Their brick-and-mortar location has given Sanguich the opportunity to invite people into their space and provide an atmosphere that matches the food, which still takes center stage. Beginning with six sandwiches, Sanguich filled out its menu with *croquetas,* "Cuban nachos," and *batidos.* As a forward-thinking business, Sanguich may be the first Cuban restaurant in Miami to offer anything vegan, let alone a sandwich. With the recent success of the meatless hamburgers, they decided to develop their own meatless *lechón,* with one condition, "It had to be real *Cubano,*" Daniel said. "It took us a long time because Rosa and I are not chefs, so we really have to study it." Jackfruit tends to absorb the flavors it is exposed to. They treat it more or less like *lechón,* using a slow-roasted garlic and onion confit to impart a strong base of flavor. Cooked on the flattop, the jackfruit filling is topped with pickled onions and their signature garlic mojo sauce. They even make a Cuban bread that utilizes olive oil instead of lard.

For dessert, Sanguich has mixed up their batido (fruit/milkshake) program. Inspired by the flavors of her childhood, Rosa combined the flavors of the *timba,* a miniature after-dinner sandwich made with guava, cream cheese, and Cuban crackers, into one dreamy beverage. After days of trial and error, she finally perfected Sanguich's guava and cream cheese milkshake. Sanguich's unique offerings are now available nationally, as they ship their own line of pickles, mustard, and sauces. For those craving the full experience, Goldbelly ships boxed kits that contain all the ingredients to assemble your own Sanguiches. The business has already outgrown the space and will soon occupy a much larger location.

"The Cuban sandwich meant a lot to me and my community," Daniel reflected, "but I had no idea the amount of awareness outside our state. I pride myself in knowing that we are the most consistent Cuban sandwich shop in the country."

Andrew Tambuzzo,
The Boozy Pig (Tampa)

Perched atop an aluminum stool at the counter of his Tampa butcher shop and deli, The Boozy Pig, Andrew Tambuzzo pauses when asked: How long did it take to create El Mixto, his version of a Cuban sandwich?

It's not an easy answer. From one point of view, it took four years of research. From another, it took most of his life. Four years ago, Tambuzzo relocated outside Asheville, NC, from Tampa to help an uncle operate Nico's Cafe, a small sandwich shop that featured Tampa-style entrees such as palomilla steaks. Although Tambuzzo had worked in places like Sweet Tomatoes and Steak & Ale, this was his first real cooking job. On the menu was a sandwich that included roasted pork marinated in traditional Cuban mojo. Also on the menu at Nico's: A Tampa-style Cuban sandwich.

"I'd always try to get him to put the mojo pork on the Cuban," he said. His Uncle usually opted for sliced deli pork instead, the way most other restaurants typically do.

"Come on, let's try it," Tambuzzo begged. "We tried it, it was better, but it didn't make sense moneywise. So he never did it." The idea went into his mental recipe box.

Years later, Tambuzzo moved back to Tampa and started getting into all types of butchery, including charcuterie, curing, brining, and smoking. He began taking sausage-making and butchering courses online while devouring whatever books he could find. He was consumed by mastering all there was to know about old-school cuts and how to make proteins better with an expert slice or filet.

"I stepped in the rabbit hole and I'm still falling," he said.

It was a curiosity innately born from family heritage. The son of a Sicilian and Cuban father and a Sicilian mother, Tambuzzo learned to make Italian sausage at about age eight from his grandfather, Giuseppe "Joe" Tambuzzo. Joe learned the family's sausage recipe after returning home from World War II and going to work with his brothers at a provisions store in east Ybor City, a Tampa neighborhood created in the late 1800s for cigar factory workers. Later, when Joe and a friend decided to open their own store in Ybor City, Tip Top Grocery, fresh-made pork sausage was their specialty.

By the time Andrew was born, his grandfather was semiretired, but he would still visit the shop and make sausage. Mainly, he was making it to sell to the guys he was playing cards and dominos with at Centro Asturiano, a social club for descendants of immigrants from Asturias, Spain. Wherever his grandfather went, Andrew would tag along.

"I was the young kid with all the old men," he remembers. "As soon as I got bored, it was like, 'Here's an empty Scotch bottle. Go play with it. Go break it.' An old .38 that didn't work anymore? 'Go play with this.'"

When he got old enough, his grandfather said, "Here's a knife. Go cut up that piece of pork." Nothing specific. Just cut it into pieces. Do anything other than bother his grandfather. Then every time there was a Christmas or summer break, he'd hang with his grandfather. "He'd take me to go pick up meat. He'd take me to go get the spices. He'd take me to go learn how to pick out parsley."

He got a kids-eye-view through the back doors of Tampa Steak Company and City Meat Company, little places around town where he'd watch butchers in white coats and hard hats and boots. "Put your hands in your pocket," he was told. "Don't touch nothing," he was told. He followed directions. Sausage making skipped a generation in the family, with Andrew's father Marcello more interested in woodworking than food. But when Joe got tired of making sausage, Marcello learned to preserve the family tradition.

When Andrew returned to Tampa from Asheville in 2016 to pursue becoming a firefighter and emergency medical technician, he remembered what he learned about sausage growing up. That reignited the ideas he had in North Carolina about different ways to prepare the roasted pork.

Instead of the sour orange mojo, Tambuzzo thought about what his Sicilian grandmother did in Ybor City, where Italian and Spanish cultures mingled. Her mojo skewed Italian with fresh herbs, lots of garlic and olive oil, but then opted for red wine vinegar as a tenderizer instead of the acid from sour orange juice. Tambuzzo began making the mojo pork every once in a while for family get-togethers or someone's birthday. He focused on refining his technique for cooking the coppa, the prized extension of the loin in the pork shoulder that is more marbled and flavorful.

Enter ham. He researched ways to cure, first dunking the entire ham with the skin on and bone intact with very few trims. As time went on he learned tricks about deboning, how Italian butchers might make culatello, fiocchi, or boneless prosciutto hams so that the curing brine could penetrate deeper. Then he experimented with smoking to determine the right length of time to get the flavor dimensions he wanted.

Years passed until he was finally satisfied.

"At that point, I realized I was halfway to a Cuban sandwich," Tambuzzo said.

Third-generation Tampa butcher Andrew Tambuzzo invested four years of research and experiments to create the Mixto sandwich for his meat market/restaurant, The Boozy Pig. "I stepped in the rabbit hole and I'm still falling," he said. Chip Weiner Photographic Arts.

"I had the mojo pork, and the ham was only getting better every time I did it. Let me work on salami."

He wasn't quite sure how to ferment and cure salami, but his experience making sausage as a boy flattened his learning curve. He essentially just wanted a wide-diameter sausage that was tasty.

After finding the right beef casing, he changed a few things in the family recipe, flip-flopping the ratios of beef to pork because he had more beef trim available after butchering cows. It took months to find out the right combination after hanging the salami in the cooler so that the casing was able to dry properly before being smoked. Incorrectly prepped salami resulted in tiger stripes while smoking.

"It was a hell of a lot easier than the pork and the ham, I can tell you that, because I was already comfortable making sausage and stuffing and curing the sausages," he said. "It was only just a few edits between the first and second batch and we're still running that second batch recipe."

For the sandwich's pickles, Tambuzzo started making them himself at home, then ran into a time crunch because he was busy by then making sausage from home for local restaurants. After talking with a cousin who is a chef, he arranged for the pickles and mustards to be made to his recipe.

At The Boozy Pig in Tampa, Andrew Tambuzzo had fashioned a *mixto* with house-made Italian-style cold cuts on Cuban bread, including salami.

Even mustard got the Tambuzzo treatment. Not one to waste, he used the juice from the dill pickles originally to make the mustard. When that was determined to be a little too strong, he had his cousin make a straight up yellow mustard. He mixed that with a bacon fat mayonnaise to create an aioli for the sandwich.

What didn't get tweaked: The Swiss cheese and Cuban bread from the century-old La Segunda Central Bakery in Ybor City, sliced corner-to-corner on a bias to get that easy-to-eat angle.

"My dad would always say, 'To get a good bite, you almost had to stab yourself in the back of the throat.' I tell the guys in the kitchen all the time, 'If it's not corner-to-corner, just give it to the dishwasher or I'll eat it. That's on the recipe and procedure. Even our Breakfast Cuban is corner-to-corner. Any sandwich on Cuban bread, corner-to-corner."

In March 2019, when he opened The Boozy Pig on Cypress Street in Tampa, Tambuzzo finally created the sandwich he wanted, but was adamant about not calling it a Cuban sandwich. Instead, the black chalkboard menu reads, "El Mixto." Calling a Cuban sandwich by name in Tampa restricts how much you can change the basic formula. Tambuzzo's sandwich was born of curiosity and experimentation.

Reactions varied. Some customers were looking for the subdued flavor profile of what they had at other shops, then they realized all the meats were house-made.

"I wasn't calling it a Cuban, I was calling it a mixto," he said. "I was very cautious of how we described it. This is *our* version of how we do a Cuban."

7

Going Global

The Cuban Sandwich Crisis of 2012

Bored with the humdrum hamburger in the 1990s and early 2000s, consumers in the United States sought out toasted and hot-pressed sandwiches such as the *panini*. As interest in the Cuban sandwich increased, the public debate over its origins and variations intensified. *Road Food* journalists Jane and Michael Stern visited Miami in 1991 and did a little research to settle the issue. They claimed the Cuban sandwich was "invented" by José Sacre in the 1940s at the Cedars of Lebanon Cafetería in Artemisa (about forty miles from Havana), but it wasn't discovered in the United States until the 1960s. After the Sterns left for their next stop, questions still lingered in Florida's humid air.

Tampa Tribune writer Ann McDuffie was incredulous at the story sold by the Sterns.

> When the group of girls and boys I grew up with became old enough to date, we used to go out to Ybor City after dances and other special events to eat Cuban sandwiches, and sometimes garbanzo bean soup, too, before going home. We liked the pressed sandwiches, the ones flattened while being heated. I always supposed that these distinctive taste treats are called Cuban sandwiches because they originated in the country so close to Florida shores. Now I've read in the *New York Times* that the credit for originating the Cuban sandwich goes to a man named Jose Sacre, who arrived in Cuba from Lebanon in the 1930s, and ten years later opened the Cedars of Lebanon Cafeteria in Artemisa west of Havana. Well, it just can't be true. I know that I was eating Cuban sandwiches as early as the 1940s.[1]

In 1997, *Tampa Bay Times* journalist Jacquin Sanders inquired about the history of the Cuban sandwich but found little. Even Florida historian extraordinaire Dr. Gary Mormino was stumped by the question, and that doesn't happen often.[2]

While national publications had usually referred to Miami as the birthplace of the Cuban sandwich, some sandwich partisans in Tampa pointed out the older pedigree of their bread and addition of salami. In 2006, Andrew Huse (the historian who led this book project) wrote an article in a local magazine that disputed the narrative told in the press. In the article, he claimed the Cuban sandwich's lineage ran deeper in Tampa than in Miami. Huse also wondered what the handcrafted sandwiches of old would have tasted like, declaring he would pay twenty dollars for a great specimen. When the article was republished in *Cornbread Nation 5: The Best of Southern Food Writing* several years later, its message went national.

The exact composition of the sandwich was never settled because it was always a matter of preference, of time and place, the kind of casual debate that peppered smoky games of dominoes. That is, until 2012, when long-simmering intermunicipal conflict over the Cuban sandwich's "home" became a minor media sensation.

Every good news story requires a conflict, and this one broke out over an announcement made by Tampa's City Council. Member Yvonne Yolie Capin saw the sandwich's history in Tampa as a marketing opportunity. She proposed a resolution that enshrined the Cuban as Tampa's official sandwich, calling for ham, roast pork, and salami on Cuban bread with pickles and Swiss cheese.

On April 19, 2012, when the council unanimously passed her resolution, Miami's sandwich partisans erupted with laughter and Spanish expletives, while its mayor waved off the notion, strangely insisting that salami is fit only for pizzas.

With the Republican National Convention planned in downtown Tampa later that year, the Cuban sandwich story became part of the city's publicity blitz. The culinary credibility of Tampa's City Council was called into question months later, when it tried to grab more headlines by claiming bacon as a distinctive local ingredient. Council dubiously announced that a conquistador's march through the Tampa area in the 1500s was somehow responsible for bacon's presence in North America. Everyone ignored that lame grab at headlines, but the intercity rivalry over the sandwich resonated.

The press had some fun with the story for a while, prompting a round of debates, origin stories (all taking place in the 1950s or 1960s), memories, and opinions. Of course, neither city would consider a change in their local preferences.

In the *Miami Herald,* Fabiola Santiago wrote, "Tampa has some serious pedigree when it comes to keeping history but no culinary chops. They let a salami slip into their Cubano sandwich. Next thing you know, they'll be adding a slice of turkey." In the process of trying to mock Tampa's claim, Santiago had inadvertently identified the old favorite with turkey joining the *salchichón* or salami. This four-meat version of the sandwich was popular in Cuba and Tampa as recently as the 1950s.[3]

Andres Viglucci offered a thoughtful assessment, concerned more with the quality of the sandwich than its exact composition or provenance.

> The Tampa resolution has landed, among those Miamians who take such matters very seriously, like a shot across the bow of exile pride, rekindling an old debate about the cloudy origins of the *sandwiche* Cubano and—*por supuesto*—who makes the best one. Or whether it's even possible to get a good Cubano anymore, in either city, as sandwich makers increasingly resort to cheap ingredients like boiled ham instead of glazed, and processed pork in place of slow roasted, mojo-steeped *pierna,* or bastardizations for the American palate like lettuce, tomato and mayo, as in the version sold in some places in Key West and Tampa. Virtually everyone agrees that it's hard to find one in Cuba.[4]

For his part, Enrique Fernández shared several nuances to the sandwich's history and ingredients.

> Having lived in Tampa from 1957 to 1964, I can attest that the Cuban sandwiches rocked. Not just Miami but all of south Florida is awash in variations of the Coral Way Cafeteria—now gone—but their *Cubanos* don't measure up. In both cities, they were first made by Spanish immigrants, mostly *gallegos,* who hand-sliced home-roasted pork leg (i.e., fresh ham), home-glazed ham, also on the bone, and big rounds of Swiss cheese.
>
> Many sing the praises of Tampa's palm-frond threaded Cuban bread. I'm one of them.[5]
>
> Cuba's original *sanwiche mixto* already included something like salami. I do recall having those sandwiches as a child at a couple of places in Havana where they added, if not salami, probably a Spanish cold cut (sobrasada?) that gave the mix a nice pungency.[6]
>
> But what I would argue passionately is that the great emporium of the Cuban sandwich was The Silver Ring in Ybor City, where, in truth, I don't recall if they used salami [they did]. What may be more surprising is

that their house-roasted pork was not cooked with mojo, the Cuban garlic marinade and sauce that has become an American staple. When the storefront deli was still around, the owner revealed that their pork had no such seasoning. Years later, the father of Rosy, of the great Rosy Bakery in the Sweetwater district of Miami, told me mojo turned pork shoulder too dark while roasting, so he seasoned his with just salt and pepper and brushed mojo on the sandwiches. Curiously, that was only for *pan con lechón*—pork sandwiches. At Rosy the Cubanos don't include pork, though they're still good thanks to the bakery's terrific bread.[7]

The sandwich is contested because it is so beloved and so variable. While Tampa's history is vital, the sandwich belongs to exile Miami in ways that most people in Tampa could never fathom. The most overlooked aspect of its story is the deep heritage shared between Havana, Miami, Tampa, Key West, and other places brightened by Cuban culture. The Cuban sandwich, conceived in Cuba and adopted by the United States, truly belongs to the world now. All the world, it would seem, except for Cuba itself. Pablo Medina wrote, "A Cuban remains a Cuban in Havana, in New Jersey, and in Miami, although, ironically, in the North he gets fat on Cuban sandwiches while in Havana he can only hunger for them."[8]

The Pilgrimage

In the 2010s, as Cubans coped with the rigors of the state-led economy and everlasting embargo, tourists searched in vain for the old *mixto,* the Cuban sandwich in its natural habitat. Journalist Chris Meesey found that the sandwiches on the island weren't mixed at all. While seeking the sandwich for the *Dallas Observer,* Meesey wrote that sandwiches "will probably consist of pork or ham, the two meats never sharing the bill on the same sandwich, together with watery mustard, dismal government bread, a generic, Swiss-like cheese. And good luck finding pickles! Real Cubans are only served in the United States."[9]

Julie Cohen sought the Cuban sandwich in 2012.

I gorged myself on the world's best mangoes, learned subtle differences between household recipes for *moros y cristianos* (black beans and rice), and ate dozens of greasy, doughy peso pizzas that had been cooked and sold on the street. But I never saw a single Cuban sandwich. Sandwiches are still eaten in Cuba, of course, but they're unrecognizable from what we know them to be here in The States. If there is pork, there won't also be ham, for two meats together would be far too decadent. The cheese and bread are government-issued, pickles are impossible to find, and the mustard is the consistency of the stuff that oozed out when you forgot to shake the bottle.[10]

Tim Johnson blogged in 2016, "In *El Centro,* I asked restaurant owners and passersby alike for *el sandwich?* On the seaside Malecon, I inquired the same of young sunny-day revelers, who clustered there with a bottle of Havana Club rum and often, an old transistor radio. No dice." Tanja Buwalda, restaurateur in Havana, admitted, "You won't find a single place in this city that serves one." A man searching for Cubanos in 2017 had to settle for "a ham and cheese sandwich served with lettuce and tomato and a French roll. Blasphemy!"[11]

The *Wall Street Journal* pointed out that most Americans visiting the island wanted to eat Cuban sandwiches, but the upscale tourist restaurants in Cuba only served what they thought tourists wanted to eat. Vendors had still not figured out how famous the Cubano had recently become overseas. Families ran sandwich stalls out of the back of their homes, selling cheap morsels to fellow Cubans, usually favoring pressed ham, cheese, or mayonnaise. The conundrum: "The best restaurants aren't Cuban, and the real Cuban restaurants are not terribly good."[12]

Perhaps the culinary pilgrims were in search of the wrong Cuban sandwich all along. "There is another classic Cuban sandwich," Enrique Fernández wrote of a family favorite in the 1950s, "this one more criollo. *Pan con lechón,* a roast pork sandwich. There was *pan con lechón* all over Havana, but *el maestro* made the best my family ever had, certainly the best I've had to this day."

> We drive out of town for this one, to a community just outside Havana where, in the central plaza, a sandwich maker whom we know by no name other than *el maestro* sells them from a cart. Inside it there is fresh ham, cooked in the Cuban manner—first marinated in garlic, sour orange juice, and possibly herbs, then slow roasted. He slices it paper thin with a knife and layers the slices on crusty Cuban bread. The meat is touched with *mojo de ajo,* a sauce with the same ingredients as the marinade, topped with the other piece of bread and given to us. In Miami, I will look in vain for a *pan con lechón* that approximates this masterpiece, but never find it.[13]

Sent by the *Wall Street Journal,* Tom Downey traveled to Cuba in search of the sandwich in 2017. He asked his driver to skip the bright tourist spots in favor of local favorites. To his surprise, they drove to La Lechonera, a roadside stand on the outskirts of Havana. There, workers carved pork from two whole roasting hogs, piled it high onto soft rolls, and garnished it with raw onions, peppers, and chili vinegar. Whereas the backdoor sandwiches of Havana cost between five and twenty cents, La Lechonera charged between a dollar and $1.60, affordable only to those lucky enough to earn convertible pesos, the currency spent by tourists. The doctor earning twenty dollars monthly would rarely, if ever, be able to afford such an extravagance.[14]

Perhaps the only Cuban sandwich most people would recognize can be found at one of the only American eateries on the island: The pub in the US Navy base at Guantanamo Bay, Cuba. The base has featured some form of the dish since the early 1980s. According to a *Miami Herald* journalist who sampled it in 2018, the sandwich is not much better than those found elsewhere on the island.[15]

Cubans traveling abroad were shocked to find that the very word "Cubano" was used to describe the most oversized dishes. While Daisy Valera visited Mexico from Cuba in 2015, she was shocked to find a so-called "Cuban"-style *torta,* or Mexican sandwich. "Mexico's Cuban sandwich is a culinary obscenity, combining breaded beef, leg of pork, chicken breast and who knows what else—a stack of meat and condiments to last two lifetimes. It baffles the Cuban who has just set foot in Mexico City, making one think that Mexicans haven't gotten wind that the nearby island is actually the home of soy mince-meat and meager chicken rations, dispensed in lieu of fish." Before the revolution, Cubans were so well-known for over-the-top culinary constructions that restaurants and food stands in Mexico call any taco with three meats *Cubano.*[16]

There is nothing more embarrassing for the revolution than the fact that Cuba's number one source of revenue is not sugar or tourism, but remittances sent to relatives from exiles, mostly in the United States. That trickle of money is often the only thing that made life bearable for those lucky enough to receive them.[17]

The state had shown little interest in reviving Cuban culinary classics until recently. The private *paladares* helped to provide some genuine Cuban cooking as an alternative to the soulless state eateries. In the late 1990s, Havana's City Historian Eusebio Leal launched a revitalization project in an attempt to bring back some of the crumbling city's old luster. The dining scene has certainly improved for tourists, and there are signs that the Cuban state is taking steps to honor the island's culinary past.[18]

In 2008, the state-run Puerto de Sagua restaurant in Havana restored the original *frita* to the menu, with fried *malanga* sticks and all. Leal, who chaired the Habaguanex state-run tourism corporation, approved reinstating the *frita* in Cuba.[19] In 2013, Habaguanex opened a newly renovated Sloppy Joe's whose namesake sandwich is *picadillo* on a hamburger bun. Even the Cuban sandwich has made furtive reappearances in Havana's dining scene.[20]

One would think that the Cuban government would capitalize on the popularity of its namesake sandwich, but the Cubano belongs to the exile. The very characteristics that set the Cuban apart: its size, the one-upmanship of employing layers of high-quality ingredients, and the care with which it is assembled and pressed, do not translate into the Communist ethos. Only the Cuban emigrants and exiles of old and their exuberant appetites, coupled with plentiful ingredients, could have fashioned the compact and everyday extravagance of the Cuban sandwich. It is downright counterrevolutionary.

While they have shared it with the world, the sandwich will always belong to the exile, and perhaps one day, to all Cubans again.

Stardom

In 2001, McDonald's got into the Cuban sandwich business, offering a new Latin-inspired menu in parts of South Florida, testing dulce de leche McFlurries, the Latin McOmelet, and pineapple-mango dipping sauce for their chicken McNuggets. Somehow the sandwich (and Cubans everywhere) was spared the indignity of being called a "McCuban." The promotion did not attract Latin customers and was quickly aborted, but just as other fast-food chains look to McDonald's when choosing locations, they are also not beyond imitating its food concepts. Blimpie's, Potbelly's, Pollo Tropical and Arby's all reassembled existing ingredients to sell Cuban sandwiches, too. Still, the market has resisted efforts to institutionalize the sandwich thus far.[21]

The Cuban sandwich's best proselytizer came from Hollywood. If the art of cinema is "history written in lightning," then the Cuban sandwich has its very own thunderbolt woven into the film *Chef,* written and directed by John Favreau. Like his character Chef Carl Casper, Favreau and consultant chef Roy Choi reveled in "food porn." Such treatment of high-brow cuisine, as in the film's early scenes, is par for the course. Yet as the plot takes a turn, Favreau spends much of the movie seducing the viewer by lovingly preparing Cuban sandwiches. The movie raised awareness of the sandwich in faraway places, but just as importantly, it sharply raised expectations about its potential. Instead of a cellophane-wrapped mediocrity, *Chef* emphatically announced to the world that the sandwich is not fast food but a dynamic dish worthy of a chef's attention. The film romanticized and celebrated the handcrafted approach to the sandwich that made it notable in the first place. The food industry responded to the message. Between 2012 and the end of 2017, the sandwich has appeared on 26 percent more menus and is known among 61 percent of consumers.

Clearly, the Cuban sandwich has crossed new boundaries. Most importantly, the sandwich's moment on the silver screen inspired chefs and amateurs across the globe to explore its intricacies. Everyone with a long piece of bread, some cold cuts, and a sandwich press is mashing up new versions, producing some playful and pleasantly surprising results. Take the unlikely JewBan. There are few things less kosher than a sandwich with several layers of pork paired with cheese and bread that may or may not contain lard. In 2017, "Jewish mother and a Cuban foodie" Julie Dana and Ray Garcia opened a food truck in Florida, JewBan's Deli Dale (pronounced *jooban's deli daaally*), serving their own spin on Cuban and Jewish deli favorites. The JewBan is a Cuban served as a bagel sandwich, and the Cuban JewBan is a Cuban sandwich with hot pastrami and coleslaw piled on. Add sauerkraut to a Cuban and you get a Cuban JewBan Reuben.[22]

Even the exiles in Miami will tolerate variations these days, as long as they don't involve salami. Michael Schwartz, the James Beard Award–winning chef and operator of Michael's Genuine restaurant, invented a Cubano-inspired pizza. He crowned his creation with ham and pork from Versailles restaurant, fontina and gruyere cheeses, pickles, and a mustard sauce. Each came garnished with a single golden-brown ham croquette gracing the center of the pizza. The announcement of the pizza met with mixed reactions online, and reviews were generally good.[23]

Local devotees might enjoy variations of the sandwich, but they will not quietly tolerate its image being abused. In 2015, it was not unusual when Tampa City Council candidate Mike Suarez appeared in campaign literature holding a sandwich. But voters did object to the fact that the Cuban clearly included lettuce and tomato, which made them question Suarez's hometown credentials. He got through the sandwich scandal and was reelected.[24]

The same year *Chef* was released, a new generation of innovative chefs reinterpreted the recipe at the South Beach Food and Wine Festival. From Miami's glitziest kitchens poured forth a plethora of deconstructed and reconstructed Cuban sandwiches, each more novel than the last, as reported by the *Wall Street Journal*:

A small puff of bread filled with a Swiss-cheese foam and topped with Iberian pork, ham and mustard that bursts in your mouth.

Bread made with foie-gras butter, pork-liver pâté, Emmental cheese and sour-orange mustard.

A "Reubencito," a decadent cross between a Cuban and a Reuben, with roast pork, pastrami, sauerkraut and truffle Thousand Island dressing.

A "Tonnato Cubano," drawing on the traditional Italian dish *vitello tonnato,* or veal with tuna sauce. It had pork loin, tuna mayonnaise, truffled dwarf peaches and pickled red onions.

Layers of roasted pork, ham, Swiss cheese and pickles wrapped in French pastry dough and served with a malted mustard sauce.

Roasted porchetta, tonnato sauce made with Sicilian tuna, Swiss cheese, Dijon mustard and pickles on Cuban-style bread.

Braised pork belly, Benton's country ham and a fried green tomato, smothered with Swiss-cheese fondue, daubed with mustard barbecue sauce and served open-face on griddled brioche.

Pork shoulder cooked in duck and pork fat, prosciutto, Gruyere cheese, cornichons (French pickles), and jalapeños.[25]

After reading through the menu of such fanciful "sandwiches," it seems clear that chefs of all persuasions are not bashful about reengineering a dish with ingredient variations, sometimes simply as an experiment. Some might scoff at McDonald's marketing its own Cuban or chefs de- and re-constructing it as some sort of exercise, but there is no greater sign of success than radical emulation, however insincere. This is what happens to every popular culinary creation in the United States, foreign and domestic: the more cherished a dish, the more it is bastardized, remixed, and mashed up. There are countless Cuban-inspired products and recipes for burgers, wraps, sliders, salads, egg rolls, bowls, omelets, macaroni and cheese, potato chips, hot dogs, pizzas, breakfast bagels, and even Cuban-Mexican *tortas.*

Still, the elite gourmet menu from the South Beach festival would probably make most sandwich fans crave the real thing, as humble as it may be. That's because the sandwich is freighted with so much more than its layers of ingredients. The Cuban defies major improvement or innovation because, when made with care and quality ingredients, it is already the most fully actualized version of itself. The devil is in the details, and there are many, because the sandwich is not composed of a handful of ingredients but a series of recipes constructed to form a whole. There is also the sense of place to consider, that immeasurable, intangible sense of authenticity when your experience—in this case a sandwich—resonates with the places and people around you. Beyond that, hidden between the thin veneers of meat, pickle, and cheese, are layers of celebration and struggle, a people's patriotism and pathos, a virtual flag of Cuban exile that flies freely across the world. Long may it reign!

The Staff of *Cook's Country*: Test Kitchen Chefs

As executive food editor for *Cook's Country* magazine, Bryan Roof's job includes traveling the country researching unique American foodways. Based on his explorations, the magazine then offers home cooks simple recipes, tips, and resources for re-creating down-home country meals.

Pierogis from Pittsburgh. St. Paul Sandwiches from St. Louis. Fried chicken from Salisbury, North Carolina. Roof investigates and devours the country's culinary roots and brings his findings back to the editorial offices in Boston, home to parent company America's Test Kitchen.

The prime candidate for discovery in 2019: The Cuban sandwich.

"It's something that everybody thinks they know," Roof said.

So Roof and senior staff photographer Steve Klise flew to Tampa that April to attend the annual Cuban Sandwich Festival in Ybor City. "It's always interesting to us when there's a festival for something," Roof said. "There's some kind of a bratwurst fest in New Braunfels, Texas. There's all these random festivals you don't know about if you're not living in that part of the country."

Before he went to Tampa, if he had a Cuban sandwich anywhere else, he didn't think twice about it. He vaguely assumed mayonnaise, lettuce or tomatoes were involved with two kinds of pork, some mustard and some pickles.

"I thought it was a Miami sandwich until I got down there and started talking to people," he said. "It would come up in conversation with complete strangers. Uber drivers and whatnot. 'You want a Cuban sandwich, you gotta go to this place or this place.' Everybody started having an opinion about it."

The first day of the festival, which was attended by thousands of Cuban sandwich fans, he didn't know which specimen to sample. He listened for mumbles, trying to glean intel from people nearby.

"I'm looking and it looks pretty good to me," Roof said.

He quickly realized people had a pretty strong opinion of what a proper Cuban sandwich was.

"I wasn't prepared for that," he said. "Once I was there and I heard people speak passionately about the sandwich, I was like, all right, we've gotta create this sandwich."

Then he and Klise interviewed Andrea Gonzmart Williams, fifth-generation owner of the Columbia Restaurant in Ybor City, and discovered how much thought went into the sandwich's ingredients and consideration of its history in Tampa.

"They've done some research," Roof remembers thinking. "They're not just saying this is the best. They've taken into consideration all these elements. Even down to the layering of the mustard.

"That became our model and sealed the deal for us," he said. "These people are fanatical about it. That's always a great story."

That's when the adventure began.

Roof began working as a test cook for *Cook's Illustrated* in 2006, was an on-screen test cook on the PBS series "America's Test Kitchen," and has worked on various magazine, book, and website projects.

The company had discussed doing a YouTube series called "The Test Cook" that would follow a test kitchen cook and pull back the curtain on what goes into testing a recipe and the intensity of the procedures. It needed to have an on-the-road aspect as well as feature a food item familiar to a lot of viewers. The Cuban sandwich ticked those boxes.

"What everyone is going to find out is that people didn't really know Cuban sandwiches the way they thought they did," Roof said. "So we thought that would be a good story to tell."

Then it came time to pick the test cook. Senior Editor Cecelia Jenkins was the right person for the task. She graduated in 2009 with a history degree from the University of Massachusetts, so she was accustomed to drilling into a topic. After working briefly for a nonprofit after graduation, she attended the Cambridge School of Culinary Arts and worked her way up to being a line cook at Island Creek Oyster Bar in Boston. She joined America's Test Kitchen in 2014.

Beyond having an interest in history, an analytical mind, and culinary experience, Jenkins also loved the Cuban sandwich. Or at least the ones she knew.

"My mom has five brothers," she said. "I remember one family reunion where my uncle made [Food Network chef] Bobby Flay's version of the Cuban. And I just thought it was the best sandwich I ever had. I think he did it on the grill. It was his interpretation. I was enamored and locked in from the beginning."

"She's a great cook," Roof said. "She can really pick away at a recipe."

"I make sure that anything I put out into the world is going to make people happy and satisfied and be something I'm going to be proud of," Jenkins said.

Beyond interpreting a recipe to make it delicious, test cooks also must find a way to make the dish simple enough for the home cook to execute confidently. This recipe not only involved roasting Cuban-style pork and baking ham to perfection

America's Test Kitchen cook Cecelia Jenkins, *left,* consults with editor Bryan Roof while creating a Cuban sandwich recipe for home cooks. They appeared in a series of videos called "The Test Cook" for *Cook's Country* magazine that followed her development of the recipe. Courtesy of America's Test Kitchen.

but also required baking homemade Cuban bread from scratch. And not all home cooks know how to bake.

Anyone who has had a Cuban sandwich in Florida knows the bread is crucial to the experience. The bread alone separates Miami and Tampa, Roof said. Tampa's bread is crusty on the exterior while having a tender crumb. Miami's version of the loaf is smooth, softer, with more spring when squeezed. Jenkins would be aiming at the Tampa version.

In the grand scheme of things, a bread recipe is hard to develop, Roof said.

During the editorial meeting when the story idea was pitched, Chief Creative Officer Jack Bishop suggested using store-bought bread. "Can't you just use a baguette?" Bishop asked.

"I almost freaked out when he said that," Roof said. "I would be fearful of ever going back to Tampa after pulling off a recipe that used a baguette."

Roof explained in the editorial meeting that Cuban bread was "a completely different animal. You'll rip your gums up trying to eat that sandwich on a baguette. It's a different crumb, a different experience altogether."

To Jenkins, substituting was nonnegotiable. "If we're going to do this, we have to do this. In the editor's minds, [they're thinking] how do you write the recipe and make it approachable?"

"A sandwich . . . is that something hard to make?" executive editor Tucker Shaw said during an episode. "It shouldn't be. And yet, it is."

"I knew it would be a heavy lift," Jenkins said.

When starting research, a test cook takes a handful of recipes that already exist to see what can be learned by comparing them. The complexity comes when a dish calls for many different ingredients to be prepared. For the Cuban, that meant finding an easy-to-bake Tampa-style Cuban loaf while also simultaneously testing cooking methods for roasted pork. Just because you can lock down a bread recipe doesn't mean that your roast pork will be equally as strong. If any one of those falls short, it's back to the drawing board the next day until all the ingredients are in harmony.

Jenkins searched for a Cuban bread recipe in the style made famous by La Segunda Central Bakery in Tampa, which Roof visited during his trip. She wanted to highlight the bread's signature qualities: golden loaves that were cottony inside and crisp on the outside. Roof also wanted to stay closer to using lard in the mixture.

One obstacle: Roof had tasted the La Segunda loaf. Jenkins had not. That was by design. An editor needs to know the ultimate version.

After much experimentation that resulted in numerous dense loaves, she consulted with Andrew Janjigian, the bread expert at sister publication *Cook's Illustrated*. He suggested kneading a "sponge" into the bread dough—a technique that calls for fermenting a portion of the bread's overall yeast, flour, and water. He also suggested covering the loaf with a disposable pan to trap steam to create a crackly, paper-thin crust.

The bread was the part of the sandwich recipe that surprised her the most.

"I had never had bread that was so shatteringly crisp but that your jaw didn't hurt from wrestling to get into it," she said. "It was cottony on the inside. When you press it, it's not like it's gummy, it's this soft, crispy, crackly texture that had a little of the pork flavor."

While juggling the bread recipe, she also started her mojo pork journey. Getting a perfect roast pork takes about four hours to cook in the oven, Roof notes. "That's not something you can just go into the kitchen and bang out." A traditional Cuban mojo marinade calls for copious amounts of garlic, oregano, cumin, and sour orange juice. But Jenkins kept producing pork butts that were exceedingly dry instead of soft, velvety, and luxurious, no matter how she adjusted temperature and cook times.

Imagine the nicest kitchen with the best cooks and ovens full of roasting pork, each with digital thermometers stuck inside to cook to exact temperatures. And then they all come out less than desired.

"At one point, I had five pork butts and they were all disappointing," she said. "Honestly, it feels like you have failed, but you have to keep your goal in mind."

The unlikely remedy: Swapping in pineapple juice for the sour orange to avoid the heavily acidic marinade's tendency to make the pork dry and chewy. She also used an overnight dry rub with salt and brown sugar to keep the protein moist during cooking and added lime and orange zest to chase a mojo-like flavor profile.

To ensure moisture, she braised the pork and then uncovered the roast to caramelize the exterior. Served on the side: A mojo sauce made with garlic and juice of limes, oranges, and pineapples.

"We didn't want to diverge from tradition, but it wasn't giving us what we wanted," Jenkins said.

"We only ended up where we did because the strong mojo marinades didn't really work for us," Roof said. "In the end we used pineapple juice because it balanced out the acidity."

Jenkins said the proof was in the reaction of the staff, which gathers each afternoon during the work week to try each other's creations.

"I know when a recipe is on track when people try it and they kind of go, "Whoa," she said.

All tallied, it took eighty Cuban loaves, thirty-four pork butts and twenty-four iterations of Cuban sandwiches to get the right balance of flavors, ease of preparation, and eating satisfaction.

The recipe includes a few tweaks that might make traditionalists frown. In addition to the pineapple juice and the late-stage mojo, there's optional mayonnaise before the sandwich gets pressed in a skillet by a heavy pot. (Roof is a mayo fan.) It also calls for using deli ham for convenience. Finally, there are no less than sixteen pickle chips, about eight times as many as most Tampa spots might serve.

"We took a little liberty . . . but we think it paid off and was worth it in the end," Jenkins said.

Response was powerful when the issue was published in December 2019 with the Cuban sandwich as the cover story and an accompanying six-part You-Tube series.

"I think people liked the series," Roof said. "A common response was, 'I had no idea this is what you guys do.' People don't realize how crazy we go to make sure it works."

For Jenkins, one reader's response stood out. A Cuban woman wrote to say that she was putting the Cuban bread recipe into her family's recipe book for her kids. The taste evoked memories of her grandparents who were Cuban. She told Jenkins nothing had ever brought that emotion so strongly for her.

"I was just completely shocked," Jenkins said. "I've had those moments, I think we all have . . . these powerful moments where we realize we're all connected through food. She made it very clear that this was one of those moments for her. I didn't know how to thank her enough. I told her, 'This is why I do this.'"

Acknowledgments

The authors would like to thank all of our distinguished interview subjects: Copeland and Tony Moré Jr, Richard Gonzmart, Claudio Rodríguez, Nicole Valls, Carlos Gazitua, Gilbert Arriaza Sr. and Gilbert Arriaza Jr., Ignacio Alfonso Jr., Norman Van Aken, Melinda Lopez, Michelle Bernstein, Dennis Martínez Miranda, Carlos Argüelles, Daniel Figueredo and Rosa Romero, Andrew Tambuzzo, and the staff of *Cook's Country*. Your stories made this project truly special.

Thanks to our peer reviewers, Dr. Luis Martínez-Fernández and Norman Van Aken, for their keen observations and helpful suggestions.

Also big thanks to Chip Weiner Photography and Doug Fornberg at Readex.

Bárbara Cruz and Andrew Huse would like to thank Dr. Gary Mormino and Donna Parrino for their wisdom over the years and guidance on this project.

Jeff Houck would like to thank Cecelia Jenkins, Bryan Roof, Michael Kilgore, Caroline O'Connor, and Sef Gonzalez.

Andrew Huse would like to thank Tim Huse for his steadfast support and the late Enrique Fernández for always keeping it real.

Notes

Introduction

1. The word seems to be derived from *lonche* (lunch) but may also descend from the word *loncha* (slice).

Chapter 1. The Pearl

1. The largest of these islands are Cuba, Hispaniola (Haiti/Dominican Republic), Puerto Rico, and Jamaica.

2. Ted. A. Henken, *Cuba: A Global Studies Handbook* (Santa Barbara: ABC-Clio 2008), 5, 38, 47, 49–51; Antoni Kapcia, *Havana: The Making of Cuban Culture* (Oxford/New York: Berg, 2005), 41; Louis A. Pérez, *Cuba between Empires, 1878–1902* (University of Pittsburgh Press, 1983), 22–23.

3. Antoni Kapcia, *Havana: The Making of Cuban Culture* (Oxford/New York: Berg, 2005), 34; Ted. A. Henken, *Cuba: A Global Studies Handbook* (Santa Barbara: ABC-Clio 2008), 38.

4. Ted. A. Henken, *Cuba: A Global Studies Handbook* (Santa Barbara: ABC-Clio 2008), 43.

5. Antoni Kapcia, *Havana: The Making of Cuban Culture* (Oxford/New York: Berg, 2005), 41, 43.

6. Antoni Kapcia, *Havana: The Making of Cuban Culture* (Oxford/New York: Berg, 2005), 41. See also Araceli Tinajero, *El Lector: A History of the Cigar Factory Reader* (Austin: University of Texas Press, 2010).

7. Christiane Paponnet-Cantat, "The Joy of Eating: Food and Identity in Contemporary Cuba," *Caribbean Quarterly* 49, no. 3 (September 2003): 22. For an excellent discussion of *ajiaco* and colonial Cuba, see chapter 6 of Luis Martínez-Fernández, *Key to the New World: A History of Early Colonial Cuba* (Gainesville: University Press of Florida, 2018). Robin Moore, "Representations of Afrocuban Expressive Culture in the Writings of Fernando Ortiz," *Latin American Music Review / Revista de Música Latinoamericana* 15, no. 1 (Spring–Summer, 1994): 32–54.

8. Ted. A. Henken, *Cuba: A Global Studies Handbook* (Santa Barbara: ABC-Clio 2008), 474–75.

9. Shannon Lee Dawdy, "Comida Mambisa: Food, Farming and Cuban Identity, 1839–1999," *New West Indian Guide* 76, no. 1/2 (2002): 49–50, 55–56.

10. Shannon Lee Dawdy, "Comida Mambisa: Food, Farming and Cuban Identity, 1839–1999," *New West Indian Guide* 76, no. 1/2 (2002): 52, 55, 49–57.

11. Christiane Paponnet-Cantat, "The Joy of Eating: Food and Identity in Contemporary Cuba," *Caribbean Quarterly* 49, no. 3 (September 2003): 16. Ortíz's etymology is that Cuban *congrí* derives

directly from a Haitian name for a rice and beans dish; he conjectures that the Haitian word was derived from a compound of the French/Haitian words *congo*, according to him "bean," and *ri(z)*, meaning "rice."

12. Ted. A. Henken, *Cuba: A Global Studies Handbook* (Santa Barbara: ABC-Clio 2008), 464

13. This book makes frequent references to Cuban "exile" communities as the best term to describe politically charged Cuban enclaves such as Miami. This is not meant to imply that every person in such communities was forcibly exiled from the island by the state, nor that all Cuban Americans were born on the island. Many Cubans fled poverty and political violence, a status that might be better described as a refugee. Others emigrated from Cuba in search of a better life and could be called emigrants/immigrants. Still, for many Cubans, the term *El Exilio* ("The Exile") has become the most commonly used term for the Cuban diaspora and resettlement communities.

14. Antonio Rafael de la Cova, "Cuban Exiles in Key West during the Ten Years' War, 1868–1878," *Florida Historical Quarterly* 89, no. 3 (Winter 2011): 289–90, 294.

15. Antonio Rafael de la Cova, "Cuban Exiles in Key West during the Ten Years' War, 1868–1878," *Florida Historical Quarterly* 89, no. 3 (Winter 2011): "Key West," 289–90, 294.

16. Louis A. Pérez, *Cuba between Empires, 1878–1902* (University of Pittsburgh Press, 1983), 28, 32–33, 34–35.

17. Joan Didion, *Miami* (New York: Simon and Schuster, 1987), 57–58; Ted. A. Henken, *Cuba: A Global Studies Handbook* (Santa Barbara: ABC-Clio 2008), 299–300.

18. Antoni Kapcia, *Havana: The Making of Cuban Culture* (Oxford/New York: Berg, 2005), 31, 48, 56, 61; Louis A. Pérez, *Cuba between Empires, 1878–1902* (University of Pittsburgh Press, 1983), 16–17, 106–8.

19. Richard Gott, *Cuba: A New History* (New Haven, CT: Yale University Press, 2004), 105; Marial Iglesias Utset, *A Cultural History of Cuba during the US Occupation, 1898–1902*, trans. Russ Davidson (Chapel Hill: University of North Carolina Press, 2011), 65–68.

20. *New York Tribune*, January 1, 1905.

21. Marial Iglesias Utset, *A Cultural History of Cuba during the US Occupation, 1898–1902*, trans. Russ Davidson (Chapel Hill: University of North Carolina Press, 2011), 65–68.

22. This slang term was used to describe North Americans in general, typically US citizens.

23. Marial Iglesias Utset, *A Cultural History of Cuba during the US Occupation, 1898–1902*, trans. Russ Davidson (Chapel Hill: University of North Carolina Press, 2011), 68.

24. *Nuevo Herald*, March 25, 1989.

25. Marial Iglesias Utset, *A Cultural History of Cuba during the US Occupation, 1898–1902*, trans. Russ Davidson (Chapel Hill: University of North Carolina Press, 2011), 54.

26. Richard Gott, *Cuba: A New History* (New Haven, CT: Yale University Press, 2004), 115.

27. Jaime Suchlicki, *Cuba: From Columbus to Castro and Beyond* (Washington, DC: Brassey's, 2002), 88–89.

Chapter 2. Sandwiches

1. *Indianapolis Star*, February 28, 1909.

2. Barra bread is a Spanish-style baguette. Quoted in *Spanish Fork Press*, March 8, 1906, *The Salina Evening Journal* (Kansas), March 10, 1908. Enrique Fernández remembered, "The breads of my childhood could be *pan de manteca*, made with lard, which is what we call Cuban bread in the US, or *pan de agua*, made with just water, like a French baguette. Many Cuban sandwich eaters prefer French bread because the meats already give off enough pork fat when heated, so *pan de manteca* would be over the top." Enrique Fernández, *Cortadito: My Wanderings through Cuba's Mutilated yet Resilient Cuisine* (Miami: Books and Books Press, 2015), 58–59.

3. Shannon Lee Dawdy, "Comida Mambisa: Food, Farming and Cuban Identity, 1839–1999," *New*

West Indian Guide 76, no. 1/2 (2002): 53; *New Orleans Times-Picayune,* March 20, 1899; *Minneapolis Journal,* February 12, 1906; *Indianapolis Star,* February 28, 1909.

4. Jono Miller, *The Palmetto Book: Histories and Mysteries of the Cabbage Palm* (Gainesville: University Press of Florida), 2021.

5. *New York Times,* April 16, 1899.

6. *New York Tribune,* January 1, 1905.

7. *New York Times,* January 18, 1903.

8. N.A.M. Rodger, *The Insatiable Earl: A Life of John Montagu, Fourth Earl of Sandwich, 1718–1982* (New York/London: W. W. Norton and Company, 1993), 78–79.

9. *St. Paul Globe,* April 6, 1896.

10. *Pittsburgh Press,* June 4, 1893.

11. English tastemakers declared that any sandwich bigger than three inches square was grotesque. Anything larger may have been confused with a working man's sandwich. *Newcastle Weekly Courant,* December 12, 1891.

12. *Willmar Tribune,* August 16, 1899 (originally printed by *New York Sun*).

13. Cuban newspaper columnists considered the word a "vulgar" or lower-class slang term, the way a schoolteacher would frown upon the usage of "ain't" by a student. The Spanish term was not considered chic enough for the upper classes.

14. *Diario de la Marina,* October 2, 1873.

15. *Diario de la Marina,* December 23, 1880.

16. *Nuevo Herald,* August 5, 1998.

17. *Nuevo Herald,* August 5, 1998.

18. Ted. A. Henken, *Cuba: A Global Studies Handbook* (Santa Barbara: ABC-Clio 2008), 463–65.

19. New York Public Library online menu collection.

20. *La Lucha,* March 15, 1908. The article mentioned all of those names. *El Mundo,* May 18, 1915.

21. *El Mundo,* March 15, 1917.

22. *El Mundo,* June 15, 1924.

23. *El Mundo,* February 17, 1924.

24. *Diario de la Marina,* February 18, 1903.

25. *Diario de la Marina,* September 25, 1921.

26. *Chicago Tribune,* April 8, 1943.

27. The German center, which would have had plenty of imported cold cuts on hand for a *lonchero.*

28. Perhaps a reference to the fact that Cuba's prettiest women could often be seen riding in the cars of wealthy Cubans and Americans.

29. *Diario de la Marina,* October 15, 1921, 14.

30. *Diario de la Marina,* June 6, 1916.

31. *El Mundo,* February 6, 1918.

32. *Missoulian* (Montana), July 26, 1898. Pink teas refer to the popular practice of upper-class women holding patriotic social events, ostensibly to support the war effort against the Spanish.

33. For a close examination of New York's often-overlooked Cuban community in the 1800s, see Lisandro Pérez, *Sugar, Cigars, and Revolution: The Making of Cuban New York* (New York: New York University Press, 2018).

34. *Times* (Richmond, Virginia), October 21, 1900.

35. *New York Tribune,* February 16, 1901; *Indianapolis Journal,* February 24, 1901; *Yale Expositor,* July 7, 2014.

36. *New York Times,* January 18, 1903; *Democrat and Chronicle,* January 25, 1903.

37. *Times-Democrat* (South Carolina), May 3, 1903.

38. *The Tennessean* (Nashville), May 12, 1935; *Tallahassee Democrat,* May 22, 1936.

Chapter 3. Cigar Cities

1. *Tampa Daily Times,* December 18, 1923.
2. *Tampa Tribune,* September 9, 1906.
3. *Attica Ledger* (Indiana), December 29, 1916.
4. *Tampa Daily Times,* January 10, 1918.
5. *Tampa Daily Times,* January 5, 1922.
6. *St. Petersburg Times,* July 2, 1924.
7. In Spanish, it is a vulgar term for the female anatomy.
8. *Miami Herald,* August 6, 2003; *Tampa Tribune,* January 21, 1923, and January 6, 1927.
9. *Tampa Tribune,* December 20, 1929, and May 10, 1930.
10. *Courier News,* September 1, 1936; *New York Times,* January 15, 1939.
11. Enrique Fernández, *Cortadito: My Wanderings through Cuba's Mutilated yet Resilient Cuisine* (Miami: Books and Books Press, 2015), 58–59.
12. *Tampa Tribune,* November 28, 1937.
13. *Tampa Tribune,* January 1, 1933.
14. *Ithaca Journal* (New York), October 4, 1934.
15. *Tampa Tribune,* July 10, 1937.
16. *Miami Herald,* May 28, 1950.
17. *Wilkes Barr Times-Leader,* October 8, 1913; *The Buffalo Enquirer,* January 7, 1919.
18. *Charlotte Observer,* October 5, 1913; *Oakland Tribune,* May 24, 1922; *St. Petersburg Times,* July 9, 1941; *Mansfield News-Journal* (Ohio), April 25, 1942.
19. *Mansfield News-Journal,* April 25, 1942.
20. *Boston Globe,* January 6, 1952.
21. *The Progress* (Clearfield, Pennsylvania), July 30, 1954; *St. Louis Post-Dispatch,* February 16, 1950; *Pittsburgh Press,* January 31, 1956; *Independent Press-Telegram* (Long Beach, California), March 9, 1958; *New York Age,* July 10, 1954.
22. *Indianapolis Star,* November 28, 1971.
23. *Tampa Times,* June 11, 1929, and August 22, 1929.
24. *Tampa Tribune,* May 28, 1957; *Orlando Sentinel,* July 7, 1957.
25. *Tampa Times,* October 10, 1947.
26. *Tampa Tribune,* July 18, 1948, June 26, 1947, November 12, 1946, and December 26, 1952.
27. *Tampa Times,* November 16, 1946.
28. *Tampa Times,* August 22, 1946.
29. Charles Spoto, Spoto Family History, unpublished manuscript; *Tampa Times,* February 25, 1960; *Tampa Tribune,* November 23, 1970.
30. *Tampa Tribune,* March 11, 1956.
31. *Tampa Tribune,* February 5, 1957.
32. *Tampa Tribune,* August 23, 1957.
33. *Tampa Times,* April 2, 1955, August 21, 1954, June 4, 1960, March 26, 1965, June 25, 1965.
34. *Tampa Times,* February 25, 1960.
35. *Tampa Times,* February 13, 1961.
36. *Tampa Tribune,* August 23, 1957.
37. *Tampa Times,* August 30, 1962, November 7, 1962, October 16, 1961, December 9, 1963.

Chapter 4. Magic Cities

1. *New York Herald,* February 19, 1922.
2. There are several myths about how Abeal earned his name, most likely a moniker given to him

by visiting bartender friends from the United States, possibly former coworkers from his years working there.

3. Beginning in the 1880s, it became fashionable for wealthy people in New York to visit the poorest parts of town to see how the lesser-fortunate lived. These "slumming" outings were often for personal amusement, and less often, for philanthropic purposes. *Dothan* (Alabama) *Eagle,* April 27, 1928.

4. *Sterling* (Illinois) *Daily Gazette,* February 9, 1926; *Daily Record* (New Jersey), July 7, 1933.

5. *Ottawa Journal,* February 24, 1926.

6. *Baltimore Evening Sun,* January 20, 1928; *Brooklyn Daily Eagle,* February 27, 1928.

7. *Green Bay News Gazette,* April 9, 1928.

8. *Mashable* (blog), May 21, 2015.

9. *Food and Wine,* June 22, 2017; *Vancouver Sun,* July 27, 2006.

10. Here, compote is a reference to fruit preserves or jam.

11. As a consumer-cased magazine, *Bohemia* explored news, culture, and politics and is the oldest magazine in Latin America. Since the revolution, the publication has served as a mouthpiece for the Cuban state. *Bohemia,* July 30, 1933, March 22, 1935.

12. *Miami Herald,* November 27, 1986.

13. *Miami Herald,* November 27, 1986.

14. *Miami Herald,* July 5, 1964, November 27, 1986, December 28, 2019.

15. *Miami Herald,* August 15, 1996.

16. *Miami Herald,* November 27, 1986.

17. *Nuevo Herald,* June 24, 1993.

18. *Montgomery Advertiser,* July 6, 1952.

19. *Brownsville Herald,* March 6, 1941.

20. *Poughkeepsie Journal,* March 8, 1948.

21. *Daily Independent,* March 13, 1955.

22. *Orlando Evening Star,* February 3, 1938.

23. Antoni Kapcia, *Havana: The Making of Cuban Culture* (Oxford/New York: Berg, 2005), 91.

24. Richard Gott, *Cuba: A New History* (New Haven, CT: Yale University Press, 2004), 131; Cornelia Escher, "Performing Tropicality: The Tropicana Cabaret in Havana," *Journal of Urban History* (2019): 980–84.

25. *Detroit Free Press,* November 21, 1954.

26. Ted. A. Henken, *Cuba: A Global Studies Handbook* (Santa Barbara: ABC-Clio 2008), 93, 142.

27. *Miami Herald,* May 28, 1950; June 2, 1951.

28. Enrique Fernández, *Cortadito: My Wanderings through Cuba's Mutilated yet Resilient Cuisine* (Miami: Books and Books Press, 2015), 41.

29. Enrique Fernández, *Cortadito: My Wanderings through Cuba's Mutilated yet Resilient Cuisine* (Miami: Books and Books Press, 2015), 60.

30. José Moreno, *Before Fidel: The Cuba I Remember* (Austin: University of Texas Press, 2007); Project MUSE, https://muse.jhu.edu/.

31. Christina D. Abreu, "Cubans in Miami's Pan-American Paradise," in *Rhythms of Race: Cuban Musicians and the Making of Latino New York City and Miami, 1940–1960* (Chapel Hill: University of North Carolina Press, 2015), 190. *Nuevo Herald,* July 29, 1993. Later, a baker named Iglesias was located on Eighth Street, between Fourth and Sixth Avenues, and another established his bakery, Murguia, on Eighth and Twenty-first North West, and both began supplying bread to several of the restaurants.

32. *Miami Herald,* May 28, 1950, July 18, 1946; Christina D. Abreu, "Cubans in Miami's Pan-American Paradise," in *Rhythms of Race: Cuban Musicians and the Making of Latino New York City and Miami, 1940–1960* (Chapel Hill: University of North Carolina Press, 2015), 195.

33. Christina D. Abreu, "Cubans in Miami's Pan-American Paradise," in *Rhythms of Race: Cuban Musicians and the Making of Latino New York City and Miami, 1940–1960* (Chapel Hill: University of North Carolina Press, 2015), 190–92, 199.

34. *Nuevo Herald,* July 29, 1993.

35. *Miami News,* January 8, 1932; *Miami Herald,* September 1, 1949.

36. *Miami News,* June 14, 1953. The Miami Restaurant was situated on one of the busiest intersections in Havana.

37. *Detroit Free Press,* October 17, 1954.

38. *Miami News,* December 29, 1958

39. *Miami News,* May 27, 1958 (reprint from Saturday review); *Boston Globe,* January 10, 1965. Louis A. Pérez, *On Becoming Cuban: Identity, Nationality, and Culture* (Chapel Hill: University of North Carolina Press, 2012), 331, 335–36; Antoni Kapcia, *Havana: The Making of Cuban Culture* (Oxford/New York: Berg, 2005), 91; Christiane Paponnet-Cantat, "The Joy of Eating: Food and Identity in Contemporary Cuba," *Caribbean Quarterly* 49, no. 3 (September 2003): 20.

40. Jaime Suchlicki, *Cuba: From Columbus to Castro and Beyond.* (Washington, DC: Brassey's, 2002), 118–19.

41. T. J. English, *Havana Nocturne* (New York: William Morrow, 2007), 67. Batista eventually absconded with $300 million (valued at $2.7 billion in 2020) of his people's hard-won currency to live in isolated luxury.

42. Jaime Suchlicki, *Cuba: From Columbus to Castro and Beyond* (Washington, DC: Brassey's, 2002), 145.

43. Jaime Suchlicki, *Cuba: From Columbus to Castro and Beyond* (Washington, DC: Brassey's, 2002), 132.

44. *New York Sun,* March 23, 1952.

45. *Lubbock Morning Avalanche,* March 22, 1958.

Chapter 5. Exile and Resilience

1. *Asbury Park Press Sun,* January 11, 1959.

2. *El Paso Herald,* January 21, 1959.

3. *Chicago Tribune,* October 12, 1959.

4. *Freeport Journal,* March 2, 1959.

5. Ted. A. Henken, *Cuba: A Global Studies Handbook* (Santa Barbara: ABC-Clio 2008), 68; *Tampa Tribune,* August 14, 1959.

6. María Cristina García, *Havana USA: Cuban Exiles and Cuban Americans in South Florida, 1959–1994* (Berkeley: University of California Press, 1996), 16; *Pittsburgh Press,* April 30, 1961.

7. *Detroit Free Press,* August 15, 1960; *Tampa Daily Times,* October 4, 1960; *Orlando Sentinel,* January 15, 1961; *Tampa Tribune,* August 17, 1962. *Ft. Lauderdale News,* December 8, 1962; *Tampa Daily Times,* January 30, 1963.

8. *Tampa Daily Times,* January 11, 1961, January 30, 1963; *St. Petersburg Times,* June 13, 1963.

9. *Kansas City Times,* November 2, 1962.

10. *Palm Beach Post,* September 15, 1963.

11. Ted. A. Henken, *Cuba: A Global Studies Handbook* (Santa Barbara: ABC-Clio 2008), 76; Richard Gott, *Cuba: A New History* (New Haven, CT: Yale University Press, 2004), 167, 170, 171; Antoni Kapcia, *Havana: The Making of Cuban Culture* (Oxford/New York: Berg, 2005), 125.

12. Richard Gott, *Cuba: A New History* (New Haven, CT: Yale University Press, 2004), 187.

13. *Springfield News-Leader,* April 30, 1960; Marifeli Pérez-Stable, *The Cuban Revolution: Origins, Course and Legacy* (New York: Oxford University Press, 2012), 93, 109, 161.

14. Christiane Paponnet-Cantat, "The Joy of Eating: Food and Identity in Contemporary Cuba," *Caribbean Quarterly* 49, no. 3 (September 2003): 20, 23–24.

15. María Cristina García, *Havana USA: Cuban Exiles and Cuban Americans in South Florida, 1959–1994* (Berkeley: University of California Press, 1996), 17; Antoni Kapcia, *Havana: The Making of Cuban Culture* (Oxford/New York: Berg, 2005), 121–22.

16. Timothy Naftali, "The Blind Spot" (C-Span lecture), July 21, 2005.

17. *Standard-Speaker* (Hazleton, Pennsylvania), April 22, 1970; *Miami News*, September 9, 1959.

18. *Miami News*, November 14, 1962.

19. *Miami News*, February 27, 1964.

20. Christina D. Abreu, "Cubans in Miami's Pan-American Paradise," in *Rhythms of Race: Cuban Musicians and the Making of Latino New York City and Miami, 1940–1960* (Chapel Hill: University of North Carolina Press, 2015), 194; *Miami News*, February 27, 1964.

21. *Journal News*, December 1, 1964.

22. *Miami Herald*, May 8, 2013.

23. *Miami Herald*, August 23, 2007, April 14, 2012.

24. *Miami Herald*, October 26, 1975; *Tropic*, October 26, 1975.

25. *Miami Herald*, October 30, 1977.

26. *Miami Herald*, October 30, 1977.

27. *Nuevo Herald*, July 2, 1986, August 13, 1987.

28. As observed by sociologist Lisandro Pérez, although federal programs attempted to relocate Cuban refugees around the country, many "trickled back" to the Miami-Dade area. *Tropic*, July 14, 1974; *Miami Herald*, June 15, 1973; María Cristina García, *Havana USA: Cuban Exiles and Cuban Americans in South Florida, 1959–1994* (Berkeley: University of California Press, 1996), 44; Lisandro Pérez, "Cubans in the United States," *The Annals of the American Academy of Political and Social Science* 487 (1986): 126–37. http://www.jstor.org/stable/1046058.

29. *Nuevo Herald*, January 14, 1989.

30. *Nuevo Herald*, August 10, 1985.

31. *Nuevo Herald*, July 29, 1993.

32. *Nuevo Herald*, July 22, 1993.

33. *Nuevo Herald*, August 7, 1990.

34. *Nuevo Herald*, December 10, 1988.

35. *Nuevo Herald*, September 30, 1993.

36. *Nuevo Herald*, January 14, 1989.

37. *Nuevo Herald*, July 29, 1993; Humberto Vázquez García, *The Government of the Cubanidad* (Santiago de Cuba: Editorial Oriente, 2005).

38. *Nuevo Herald*, August 15, 1992, January 2, 1988.

39. *Nuevo Herald*, March 3, 1991.

40. *Nuevo Herald*, July 22, 1993.

41. *Nuevo Herald*, July 22, 1993.

42. *Miami Herald*, January 20, 1985.

43. *Miami Herald*, January 20, 1985.

44. *Miami Herald*, April 20, 2012.

45. *New York Times*, June 14, 1989.

46. *New York Times*, February 6, 2002.

47. *Nuevo Herald*, September 30, 1993, February 29, 1996, May 16, 1996, May 24, 1996.

48. *Nuevo Herald*, January 12, 1991, August 16, 2013.

49. *Nuevo Herald*, April 7, 1990, March 4, 1995.

50. *Nuevo Herald*, August 13, 2008.

51. *Nuevo Herald*, August 16, 2013.

52. *New York Times*, February 6, 2002.

Chapter 6. Feast and Famine

1. Antoni Kapcia, *Havana: The Making of Cuban Culture* (Oxford/New York: Berg, 2005), 149; María Cristina García, *Havana USA: Cuban Exiles and Cuban Americans in South Florida, 1959–1994* (Berkeley: University of California Press, 1996), 61.

2. *Miami Herald,* April 28, 1980, April 24, 1980, May 8, 1980.

3. *Miami Herald,* August 26, 1981.

4. *Miami Herald,* November 6, 1980; *New York Times,* November 25, 1984, December 14, 1986.

5. *Miami Herald,* December 4, 1980.

6. *New York Times,* December 14, 1986.

7. *Miami Herald,* November 17, 1979, November 10, 1979.

8. *Miami Herald,* November 29, 1979.

9. *Miami Herald,* November 28, 1979, December 4, 1980.

10. C. Peter Ripley, *Conversations with Cuba* (Athens: University of Georgia Press, 1999), 81.

11. *Palatka Daily News* (Florida), July 5, 1978.

12. In Tampa, favorites of the 1970s and '80s included the Columbia, Cuervo's, the Alvarez, JD's Soup and Sandwich, Hugo's, Obi's, La Tropicana, and Spanish Park. Miami's contest chose Versailles, Badias, Casablanca, Segundo Vijante, Salon Tropical, Floridita, Esquina de Tejas, and Las Culebrinas. *Miami News,* September 12, 1975; *Miami Herald,* November 28, 1979, December 4, 1980; *Tampa Tribune,* June 14, 1985; *Tampa Times,* October 23, 1979. Font may have been referring to Randy's restaurant (Twentieth Street and Seventh Avenue) that sold "Cuban sandwiches with Tally Slop," which turned out to be a variation on a meatball sub (*Tally* referring to "Italian") rather than a Cuban sandwich. The owner named his sandwich after the Cuban simply to attract attention, he said.

13. His Jewish parents had fled the Soviet Union, landing in Matanzas, Cuba, where Benes was born in 1934. Raised in an upper-class household, Benes was accustomed to being an outsider, since his Jewish heritage prevented him from joining any of the "Big Five" exclusive social clubs that defined Cuba's elite. After getting involved in humanitarian causes as a student of law in Havana, he also came to oppose Batista's rule in the 1950s. When Castro seized power, Benes worked briefly for the Ministry of Finance but fled the country in 1960 when he was disturbed by the excesses of the regime, including the expropriation of his father's long-standing underwear business. Robert M. Levine, *Secret Missions to Cuba: Fidel Castro, Bernardo Benes, and Cuban Miami* (New York: Palgrave MacMillan, 2002), 184–87.

14. Spurred by fears that Castro's regime would force children into indoctrination centers, Cuban parents clandestinely sent about fourteen thousand unaccompanied children to the United States on commercial flights between 1960 and 1962.

15. Robert M. Levine, *Secret Missions to Cuba: Fidel Castro, Bernardo Benes, and Cuban Miami* (New York: Palgrave MacMillan, 2002), 106–7.

16. If the exiles aren't ethnically and politically homogeneous, they often thought of themselves that way. In 1990, only 1.5 percent of Miami Cubans identified as black. Exile Miami "had a little Havana rather than a little Cuba," excluding the notion of the darker, poorer nation they had left behind. The trauma of exile gave rise to powerful far-right forces that set the tone for exiles everywhere. Cuba became an "abstract idea" scrubbed of imperfections. For all of the energy devoted to condemning and undermining Castro, these efforts did not deliver any appreciable benefits to the exiles or Cuban relatives. Being a one-issue community drowned out discussion about any other issue in town. It also made Cuban Miami remarkably insular. Robert M. Levine, *Secret Missions to Cuba: Fidel Castro, Bernardo Benes, and Cuban Miami* (New York: Palgrave MacMillan, 2002), 218–21.

17. "I feel sorry for the Cuban community in Miami," Benes once said. "Because they have imposed on themselves the same condition that Castro has imposed on Cuba: total intolerance. And ours is worse because it is entirely voluntary." Robert M. Levine, *Secret Missions to Cuba: Fidel Castro, Bernardo*

Benes, and Cuban Miami (New York: Palgrave MacMillan, 2002), 186–87, 198, 209, 219; María Cristina García. *Havana USA: Cuban Exiles and Cuban Americans in South Florida, 1959–1994* (Berkeley: University of California Press, 1996), 150.

18. *New York Times,* February 24, 1991.

19. *Miami Herald,* June 2, 1988.

20. *New York Times,* February 6, 2002.

21. "The real Cuban [sandwich] has all but disappeared from view," a reader wrote to a *Tampa Tribune* columnist in 1997. "Nowadays you're likely to get a sandwich with American processed cheese or with salad dressing or who-knows-what on it. You've got to do something!"

22. More than a million people traveled to Cuba from the United States during this period. Robert M. Levine, *Secret Missions to Cuba: Fidel Castro, Bernardo Benes, and Cuban Miami* (New York: Palgrave MacMillan, 2002), 140.

23. *Miami Herald,* January 20, 1979, May 27, 1979, January 9, 1979; Susan Eckstein and Lorena Barberia, "Cuban-American Cuba Visits: Public Policy, Private Practices," MIT Center for International Studies, January 2001, Conference: MIT, The Inter-University Committee on International Migration, Cambridge.

24. *Miami Herald,* May 27, 1979.

25. Antoni Kapcia, *Havana: The Making of Cuban Culture* (Oxford/New York: Berg, 2005), 126, 149.

26. Ted. A. Henken, *Cuba: A Global Studies Handbook* (Santa Barbara: ABC-Clio 2008), 300–301; María Cristina García. *Havana USA: Cuban Exiles and Cuban Americans in South Florida, 1959–1994* (Berkeley: University of California Press, 1996), 52.

27. Fred Ward, *Inside Cuba Today* (Crown Publishers, New York, 1978), 22.

28. Enrique Fernández, *Cortadito: My Wanderings through Cuba's Mutilated yet Resilient Cuisine* (Miami: Books and Books Press, 2015), 39–40, 73–74.

29. *Orlando Sentinel,* January 5, 1992.

30. Fred Ward, *Inside Cuba Today* (Crown Publishers, New York, 1978), 26.

31. Hanna Garth, "They Started to Make Variants: The Impact of Nitza Villapol's Cookbooks and Television Shows on Contemporary Cuban Cooking," *Food, Culture and Society* 17, no. 3 (2015): 364.

32. *The Salt,* National Public Radio, June 16, 2016.

33. Hanna Garth, "They Started to Make Variants: The Impact of Nitza Villapol's Cookbooks and Television Shows on Contemporary Cuban Cooking," *Food, Culture and Society* 17, no. 3 (2015): 372.

34. Dame Cacao, "Cuban Food in Cuba: The Complete Guide," October 13, 2016, last updated July 15, 2019 (Damecacao.com/cuban-sandwich-exist-cuba); Yenisel Rodriguez, *Havana Times,* December 1, 2014.

35. Christiane Paponnet-Cantat, "The Joy of Eating: Food and Identity in Contemporary Cuba," *Caribbean Quarterly* 49, no. 3 (September 2003): 11–29.

36. *Tampa Tribune,* November 27, 2006; *Kansas City Star,* July 8, 2004; *The Economist,* July 24, 2008.

37. Ivan Darias Alfonso, "We Are What We Now Eat: Food and Identity in the Cuban Diaspora," *Canadian Journal of Latin American and Caribbean Studies* 37, no. 74 (2012): 174.

38. *Havana Times* (blog), February 24, 2012, September 10, 2014.

39. *Cuba Trade and Investment News* 8, no. 12 (December 2006); *Havana Times,* March 2, 2011; Damecacao.com/cuban-sandwich-exist-cuba (blog), October 13, 2016.

40. Suzanne Bost and Frances R. Aparicio, *The Routledge Companion to Latino/a Literature* (London: Routledge, 2014), 258.

41. Ben Corbett, *This Is Cuba: An Outlaw Culture Survives* (New York: Basic Books, 2014), 126.

42. He only gave his first name to his interviewer to avoid being punished by state inspectors.

43. *Wall Street Journal,* April 19, 2017; Ben Corbett, *This Is Cuba: An Outlaw Culture Survives* (New York: Basic Books, 2014), 98.

44. *New York Times,* November 22, 1998.

45. Maxine Shen, "Fidel Castro's Private Chefs Tell You Where to Eat in Havana," *Food and Wine*, February 16, 2017.

Chapter 7. Going Global

1. *Tampa Tribune,* June 22, 1989.
2. *Fort Myers News-Press,* February 7, 1991.
3. *Miami Herald,* April 17, 2012.
4. *Miami Herald,* April 14, 2012.
5. *Enrique Fernandez in Black and White* (blog), February 15, 2018.
6. *Enrique Fernandez in Black and White* (blog), February 15, 2018.
7. *Enrique Fernandez in Black and White* (blog), February 15, 2018.
8. "In Search of the Elusive Cuban Sandwich," *Miami Herald,* April 14, 2012; "The Mystery of the Cuban," *Tampa Bay Times,* October 20, 1997; Pablo Medina, "The Tampa Cubans and the Culture of Exile," *Antioch Review* 62, no. 4 (Fall 2004): 635–43.
9. Chris Meesey, "For an Authentic Cuban Sandwich, Stay Away from Cuba," *Dallas Observer*, February 23, 2010.
10. Julie Cohen, "Bay of Pigs," *Sauce,* April 1, 2012, https://saucemagazine.com/a/1690/bay-of-pigs-cuba-and-americas-history-may-be-a-bit-complex-b.
11. Travel Blog by Flight Network, Tim Johnson, February 5, 2016; camilomarin, "So what do they call a Cuban sandwich in Cuba?," post on steemit, 2016.
12. *Wall Street Journal,* April 19, 2017.
13. Enrique Fernández, "Mi Paladar," *Gastronomica* 13, no. 3 (Fall 2013): 57; Enrique Fernández, *Cortadito: My Wanderings through Cuba's Mutilated yet Resilient Cuisine* (Miami: Books and Books Press, 2015), 61.
14. *Wall Street Journal,* April 19, 2017.
15. *Miami Herald,* March 30, 2018.
16. Daisy Valera, "Mexico's Cuban Sandwich," *Havana Times,* February 6, 2015.
17. Luis, p. 15 [need more info]
18. *Tampa Tribune,* January 29, 2013.
19. *Nuevo Herald*, August 16, 2013.
20. *Reuters,* April 12, 2014 (Rosa Tania Valdez); *Tampa Tribune,* January 29, 2013; *Food and Wine,* June 22, 2017.
21. *Miami Herald,* August 2, 2001; *Palm Beach Post,* October 27, 2001.
22. *Naples Daily News,* June 7, 2017.
23. *Food and Wine,* January 10, 2019; *Miami.com,* January 16, 2019.
24. *Tampa Bay Times,* March 3, 2015.
25. *Wall Street Journal,* March 21, 2014.

Index

Page numbers in *italics* refer to illustrations.

Abeal, José, 66, 156
Ajiaco, 6–7, 29–30, 93, 153
Alfonso, Evelio, 63
Alfonso, Ignacio, Jr., 62–64, 151
Alfonso, Ignacio, Sr., 62–64, *63*
Alfonso, Rafael, 62–63
America's Test Kitchen (television program),
    144–45, *146*
Antilles Islands, 5
Aparicio, Francisco, 95
Apple, R. W. "Johnny," Jr., 77–79
Argüelles, Carlos, 100–112, *111*, 151
Arriaza, Gilbert, Jr., 61–62, 151
Arriaza, Gilbert, Sr., 61–62, 151
Arroz con pollo (chicken and yellow rice), 8, 47,
    53, 74, 85

Batido (shake), 61, 82, 105, 130
Batista, Fulgencio, 75–77, 89
Beans, 8, 37, 50, 124, 138
    black, 8, 44, 94, 154
    red, 8
Beef, 6, 8, 29, 30, 31, 39, 51, 66, 70, 74, 92, 93,
    104, 109, 122, 123–24, 133, 140
Benes, Bernardo, 117–18, 160
Benítez-Rojo, Antonio, 7
Bernstein, Michelle, 84–88, 151
Bishop, Jack, 146
Bocadillo, 3, 30–31, 99
Bologna, 31, 37, 38, 92, 105, 124

Braunschweiger, 51
Bread, 3, 25, 27, 32, 33, 35–36, 37, 38, 39, 51, 57,
    67, 96, 138, 142, 157
    Cuban, 2, 3, 5, 14–17, *14*, *15*, *17*, 19, 21, *21*, 22,
        24–27, 28, 30, 38, 44, 46–47, 49, 51, 57, 59,
        60, 61–62, 64, 69, 70, 72, 73, 74, 77, 80–81,
        85, 86–88, 95, 96, 98, 99, 101, 102, 103,
        104, 106, 109, 112, 115, 116, 118, 125, 126,
        127, 130, 134, *134*, 136, 137, 138, 139, 143,
        146–47, 149, 154; and palmetto leaf, 14,
        24, 25, 26, 84
    Egg bread / Medianoche bread, 32, 52, 67,
        71, 127
    French (baguette), 24, 30, 31, 38, 51, 73, 90,
        96, 99, 118, 146, 154
    Pan de agua / water bread, 14, 25, 95, 154
    Pan de flauta (fluted loaf), 25, 33, 35, 50
    Spanish (barra), 31, 154
Bulnes, Pancho, 39–40
Butter, 1, 22, 26, *28*, 32, 35, 37, 38, 44, 51, 54,
    57, 60, 62, 64, 74, 88, 96, 102, 109, 115, 117,
    142

Cabrera, Blanca, 60
Cacciatore, Angelo, 54–55, 56
Cachaldora, Gustavo, 95
Capin, Yvonne Yolie, 136
Carro Seijido, Sebastián, 105
Castro, Fidel, 42, 60, 63, 68, 72, 77, 89–93, 94,
    95, 105, 113, 117–24, 160

Cheese, 27, 29, 30, 32, 35, 36, 37, 38, 39, 47, 49,
  50, 51, 138, 143
  American, 51, 74, 81, 96, 161
  Cream, 67, 130, 134
  Gruyere, 32, 52, 86, 142, 143
  Swiss, 1, 19, 20, 21, 35, 38, 44, 50, 52, 54, 55,
    57, 58, 59, 60, 62, 64, 69, 70, 71, 76, 80,
    81, 85, 86, 88, 90, 92, 96, 98, 100, 101,
    103, 106, 109, 112, 115, 117, 123, 125, 136,
    137, 138, 139, 142, 143; Finlandia Swiss
    cheese, 62, 64
Chef (motion picture), 42, 141, 142
Childs, George, 67, 98
Chorizo / sausage, 20, 39, 47, 49, 69, 85, 104,
  106, 117
Cigars, 6, 9, 26, 45–46, 80, 87, 109, 118, 131
Coffee, 26, 42, 44, 46, 48, 49, 69, 70, 71, 81, 90,
  93, 96, 125
Columbia Restaurant (Tampa, Florida, and
  other locations), 15, 16, 18–23, 21, 54, 56,
  144, 160
Cook's Country (periodical), 144–49, 151
Cook's Illustrated (periodical), 145, 147
Crespi, Luis, 100
Croquettes / croquetas, 12, 44, 60, 64, 117, 123,
  124, 130, 142
Cuba, 1–12, 13, 24–26, 29–39, 45–60, 61, 62,
  65–72, 75–77, 81, 82–83, 89–93, 98–100, 101,
  104–5, 107–13, 116, 118, 119–24, 135, 137–41,
  153, 154
  Agriculture, 7, 39, 121
  Independence from Spain, 3, 7–12
  Madruga, 107, 108
  Mariel Boatlift, 113–14, 117, 125
  Matanzas, 11, 62, 101, 108, 110, 160
  Placetas, 105
  Relations with the U.S., 3, 9–12, 25, 36,
    45–46, 65–66, 69, 75–77, 89–93, 113,
    117–21, 123–24, 160, 161
  Revolution, 60, 63, 89–93, 95, 101, 106, 113,
    119–24, 140–41, 157
  Slavery, 1, 6, 7, 8, 9, 29
  Tourism, 10, 47, 65, 66, 69, 70, 71, 75–76, 90,
    92, 119–20, 122, 124, 139–41
  United States citizens in, 10–12, 36, 37,
    65–66, 69–71
Cubanidad 1885 (restaurant, Las Vegas, Ne-
  vada), 107–9

Cubans
  Afro-Cubans, 3, 6, 46, 52, 110, 160
  Diet, 6–8, 92–93, 104, 106, 121–24
  Exile and exiles, 2, 3, 8–9, 24, 25, 36, 38, 41,
    44, 45, 68, 82, 89, 91, 94, 97–101, 103,
    105, 106, 113–14, 118, 119–20, 122, 126,
    137, 138, 140, 141, 142, 143, 154
Cuban sandwich
  Mixto, 1, 2, 8, 18, 32, 33, 35–38, 49, 69, 71,
    115, 131, 133, 134, 134, 137, 138
  Origins, 24–39
  Pressing and heat, 1, 2, 20, 21, 22, 28, 32, 39,
    44, 53, 55, 60, 64, 79, 80, 81, 86, 88, 95,
    103, 105–6, 109, 112, 123, 128, 135, 139,
    141, 142, 147, 148
Cuban Sandwich Factory (restaurant, Belfast,
  Ireland), 110–12

Dana, Julie, 142
Díaz, George, 121

Elena Ruz sandwich, 67–69, 97
Emparedado, 3, 30, 31, 35, 62
Estevil, Dagoberto, 105

Favreau, John, 42–43, 141
Fernández, Enrique, 48, 71, 120, 137, 139, 151,
  154
Figueredo, Daniel, 125–30, 151
Florida, 9, 13, 16, 23, 24, 39, 45–46, 47, 48–50,
  52, 55, 60, 66, 68, 72, 74, 79, 86, 98, 100, 104,
  107, 109, 116, 135–38, 141, 142, 146
Font, Jimmy, 116, 160
Frita cubana (sandwich), 94, 104–5, 140

Galindo, Luis, 101
Galindo, Raúl, 100–103, 118
Galindo, Reinaldo, 102
Garcés, Frank, 95
García, Luis, 19
García, Manuel, 47
García, Ray, 142
Garlic, 1, 8, 57, 62, 87, 99, 106, 109, 130, 147, 148
Gazitua, Carlos, 58–60, 151
Gilbert's Bakery, 61–62
Gómez, Eduardo, 115
Gómez, José Miguel, 100
González, Victoriano Benito, 105

Gonzmart, Adela, 16, 18
Gonzmart, Richard, 18–23, 151
Gonzmart Williams, Andrea, 144

Ham, 1–2, 8, *19*, 19–22, *28*, 29–33, 35–41, 44,
  47–58, 59, 62, 69–71, 76, 80–81, 84–85, 88,
  90, 92, 95, 96, 98–99, 101–3, 105, 109, 110,
  112–17, 124, 125, 127–28, 132–33, 136–39,
  142–43, 145, 148
  Bolo ham, 21, 39, 40, 59, 62
Hamburgers, 54, 58, 66, 74, 94, 104, 116, 130,
  135, 141, 143
Havana, 2, 9–11, 25–26, 30, 33–34, 37, 38, 45–46,
  47, 48, 49, 50, 65–73, *73*, 75–77, 82, 89–91,
  94–97, *97*, 99–101, 103, 105, 114, 116, 121,
  123, 128, 135, 137–41, 155, 160
  El 1830 (nightclub), 95
  Bar OK, 99–100
  El Carmelo restaurant, 67–68, 97, 117
  Cedars of Lebanon Cafetería (in Artemisa),
    135
  Club Vasco (nightclub), 70
  Flamingo (nightclub), 70
  Floridita Bar, 69, 95, 160
  La Gerona (bakery), 99
  Habaguanex (corporation), 140
  Havana Hilton (hotel), 76–77
  Hotel Nacional, 76, 90
  La Lechonera, 139–40
  Montmartre (nightclub, Havana, Cuba), 70
  El Morro (cafeteria), 101
  National Institute of Tourist Industries, 120
  Puerto de Sagua (restaurant), 105, 140
  Riviera Salon Rojo (nightclub), 70
  Royalty Cafeteria, 101
  Sagrado Corazón School, 67
  Sans Souci (nightclub), 70
  Sloppy Joe's (Cafe/Bar), 66, 76, 140
  El Templete (nightclub), 70
  Tropicana (nightclub), 70
  Vedado (neighborhood), 34, 67, 75, 95, 97,
    105
  Les Violines (nightclub), 95
  La Zaragozana (nightclub), 70
  Zombie Club (nightclub), 70
Hemingway, Ernest, 66, 69

Iyer, Pico, 124

Jenkins, Cecilia, 145–49, *147*
Jewban's Deli Dale (food truck), 142

Key West, Florida, 1, 9, 36, 37, 39, 45–46, 66, 72,
  79–81, 137, 138
  Cuban Coffee Queen (restaurant), 81
  Sandy's Cafe, 81
  Sloppy Joe's (café/bar), 66
  Tavern N' Town (restaurant), 80

Leal, Eusebio, 140
Lechón. See Pork
Lettuce, 37, 38, 49, 50–51, 53, 74, 81, 106, 117,
  118, 137, 139, 142, 144
Lleonart, Orestes, 95
Lleonart, Roberto, 95
Lonchero (sandwich man/slicer), 1, 33–36, *34*,
  55, 58, 68, 98, 100, 101, 105, 155
Lopez, Melinda, 82–83, 151

Malanga, 103, 140
Martí, José, 9
Martínez Miranda, Dennis, 107–9, 151
Mayonnaise, 37, 50, 51, 53–54, 80, 85, 88, 109,
  117, 118, 123, 130, 136–37, 139, 143, 144, 148
Medianoche (sandwich), 2, 32, 38, 51, 52, 57, 67,
  68, 82, *83*, 98, 103, 125, 127
Medina, Pablo, 138
Miami, 1, 2, 20, 21, 25, 39–44, *43*, 48, 50, 58–62,
  61, 67–68, 72–74, *73*, 77–88, *78*, *94*, 94–106,
  97, 105–9, 113–22, 125–30, *126*, 135–38, 139,
  142, 144–46, 154, 159, 160
  La Arcada (restaurant), 115
  Ayestarán Restaurant, 68, 95
  Badia Restaurant, 96, 160
  Bilbao (restaurant), 72
  Cafe La Trova, 84, 87
  Calle Ocho (Eighth Street), 42, 79, 84, 96
  La Carreta (restaurant), 42, 44, 118, 125
  Casablanca (restaurant), 95
  Centro Vasco (restaurant), 118
  Círculo Cubano (Cuban club), 72
  Continental National Bank, 115, 117–18
  Covadonga (restaurant), 72
  Do Drop Inn (restaurant), 95
  Esquina de Tejas (restaurant), 72, 118, 160
  Flamenco Supper Club, 95

Miami—*continued*
 Fontainebleau, 74
 Freedom Tower, 96
 Islas Canarias, 84
 Latin American Cafeteria, 79, 101–3, 114,
  118, 121
 Les Violines Supper Club, 95
 Little Havana, 42, 84–85, 97, 114, 128, 160
 Manchu Wok restaurants, 39
 Mesa Mar Seafood, 39
 Michael's Genuine (restaurant), 142
 Nena's (restaurant), 79
 Palacio de los Jugos, 79
 Los Pegaditos, 115
 Restaurante Habana, 72
 El Rey de Las Fritas, 105
 Rio Cristal, 79
 Rosy Bakery, 138
 Sanguich de Miami (restaurant), 125–30, 151
 Sergio's Restaurant, 58–60, 59, 125
 Son Cubano (restaurant), 109
 South Beach Food and Wine Festival, 109,
  142, 143
 El Toledo Restaurant, 100
 Versailles Restaurant, 42–44, 43, 67–69, 79,
  84, 101, 103, 113, 118, 125, 142, 160
 Yayo Cafeteria, 101
Miami Beach, 74, 79
Miami Herald / Nuevo Herald, 50, 68, 71, 72, 73,
 95, 97–100, 101, 103, 104, 114, 115, 116, 118,
 137, 140
Mojo, 1, 8, 22, 57, 81, 84, 86, 104, 106, 109, 118,
 130, 131–33, 137–39, 147–48
Montagu, John, 27
Moré, Anthony, 18
Moré, Copeland, 13–17
Moré, Juan, 18
Moré, Raymond, 18
Moré, Raymond, Jr., 18–19, 21–22
Moré, Tony, Jr., 18, 19–20
Moreno, José, 71
Mormino, Gary, 136
Morrison Meat Packers, 39–41
Mortadella, 38, 49, 98, 105
Mustard, 1, 22, 28, 29, 32, 34, 35, 39, 44, 49, 51,
 54, 57, 58, 59, 62, 64, 74, 80–81, 83, 84–85,
 88, 96, 102, 106, 109, 112, 115, 116–18, 124,
 125, 127–28, 130, 133–34, 138, 139, 142–43,
 144–45

New Jersey, 62, 63, 97, 138
 El Artesano Restaurant, 62–64
 Union City, 62–64, 63
New York City, 8, 30, 31, 35–38, 50, 60, 65, 71,
 95, 97, 102, 155, 157

Obejas, Achy, 123
Operation Pedro Pan, 82, 117
Oranges and orange juice, 1, 8, 57, 62, 69, 87,
 122, 132, 139, 142, 147–48
Orlando, Florida, 39, 70, 100
 Cervantes Restaurant, 100
 Crystal Cafe, 100
 Jimmie's Sandwiches, 100
 Joe's Sandwich Shop, 100
Ortiz, Fernando, 6, 29–30, 153–54

Pan con bistec (steak sandwich), 44
Pan con lechón (sandwich), 36, 127, 138–40
Pan con mayonesa (sandwich), 123
Paté / foie gras, 31, 32, 35, 51, 142
Peppers, 6, 140
Pérez, Ricardo, 115
Pickles (cucumber), 1, 22, 29, 34, 35, 37, 38, 39,
 44, 47–51, 54, 57, 58, 59, 60, 62, 64, 69–70, 73,
 81, 84, 86, 88, 92, 96, 98, 100–102, 106, 109,
 112, 115–18, 125, 127–28, 130, 133, 134, 136,
 138–39, 142–44, 149
Pizza, 15, 55, 74, 116, 119, 120, 123, 136, 138,
 142, 143
Plantains, 7, 8, 44, 80, 127
Pork (*lechón*), 1, 2, 8, 19, 20, 22, 31, 36, 41, 44,
 48, 49, 50, 51–52, 53, 54, 56, 57, 58–59, 62, 69,
 70, 80, 81, 82, 84, 85–88, 96, 98, 99, 101–6,
 109, 112, 114–15, 117, 122, 124, 126–28, 130,
 131–33, 136–40, 142–43, 144–45, 147–48
Puerto Rico, 8, 9, 10, 51, 153

Rice, 7–8, 10, 44, 92, 93, 94, 122, 124, 138, 154
Rodríguez, Claudio, 39–41, 41, 151
Rodríguez, Danny, 41
Rodríguez, Douglas, 109
Rodríguez, Gilda, 41
Rodríguez, José, 39
Rodríguez, Kevin, 41
Rodríguez, María Elsa, 59
Rodríguez, Yenisel, 122–23
Romero, Rosa, 125–30, 151
Roof, Brian, 144–49, 146

Russell, Joe, 66
Ruz, Elena, 66–68

Sacre, José, 135
Salami, 1, 19, *19, 20,* 22, 31, 48, 49, 50, 51, 53, 54,
    57–58, 80–81, 83, 86, 103, 105, 109, 117, 118,
    133, 134, 136–37, 142
Salchichón, 20, 31, 48–50, 105, 137
Sánchez, Rosita, 56
Sandwiches, origins of, 26–29
Santiago, Fabiola, 136
Schwartz, Michael, 142
Shaw, Tucker, 147
Sloppy Joe (sandwich), 66
Sopressata, 49
Spain, 3, 5, 7–9, 12, 30, 31, 41, 45, 57, 63, 68,
    110, 132
Spanish bean soup, 20, 47, 49, 58, 135
Spoto, Angelo, 55
Steak, 22, 25, 39, 44, 68, 69, 74, 79, 117, 123, 131
Stern, Jane, 135
Stern, Michael, 135
St. Petersburg, Florida, 22, 39
Suarez, Mike, 142
Sugar, 3, 5, 7, 12, 48, 49, 55–57, 68–69, 72, 75, 93,
    95, 121, 122, 140, 148

Tambuzzo, Andrew, 131–34, 151
Tampa, Florida, 1, 2, 13–23, 24, 26, 36–37, 39,
    45–50, *47,* 49, 53–58, 60, 72–73, 80, 81, 86,
    91–92, 103, 109, 116, 118, 119, 127, 131–34,
    133, 134, 135–38, 142, 144, 146, 147, 148, 160,
    161
    Alvarez Restaurant, 116, 160
    Gasparilla Pirate Invasion, 55
    Grand Orient Restaurant, 47
    La Segunda Central Bakery, 13–17, *14, 15, 17,*
        21, 21, 25, *134,* 147
    Silver Ring Sandwich Shop, 54–55, 137
    West Tampa, 46, 47, 48
    Ybor City, 13, *17, 17,* 137, 144
Tobacco, 5, 45, 72
Torres, Manuel, 57–58
Turkey, 19, 30–32, 35, 37–39, 47, 49–50, 53–54,
    67, 81, 96, 105, 117, 125, 137

Valera, Daisy, 140
Valls, Felipe, Jr., 42, *43*
Valls, Felipe, Sr., 42, *43*
Valls, Nicole, 42–44, *43,* 151
Van Aken, Norman, 77–81, 151
Varela y Morales, Father Felix, 8
Ventanita (service window), 18, 33, 42, *43,* 44
Viglucci, Andres, 137
Villapol, Nitza, 68, 121–22

World War I, 12, 35
World War II, 19, 50, 53–54, 72, *73,* 122, 131

Yuca, 6, 7, 8, 64

ANDREW T. HUSE is curator of Florida studies at the University of South Florida Libraries. His other books include *From Saloons to Steakhouses: A History of Tampa* and *The Columbia Restaurant: Celebrating a Century of History, Culture, and Cuisine*.

BÁRBARA C. CRUZ, a native of Cuba, is professor of social science education at the University of South Florida.

JEFF HOUCK is vice president of marketing for the Columbia Restaurant Group and previously worked as food editor, writer, and blogger for the *Tampa Tribune*.